Hymnal Studies Eight

A Scriptural Index to The Hymnal 1982

by Marion J. Hatchett

The Church Hymnal Corporation, New York

10   9   8   7   6   5   4   3   2   1

The Church Hymnal Corporation
800 Second Avenue
New York, NY 10017

Table of Contents

Acknowledgements

The Scriptural Index found in the Accompaniment Edition of *The Hymnal 1982* was the work of co-editors Jerry D. Godwin and Marion J. Hatchett. The foundational work for the project was a detailed index of *The Hymnal 1940*, compiled by Alfred Tyson in partial fulfillment of his degree from the Church Divinity School of the Pacific in 1947. Also employed was a similarly detailed scriptural analysis of the texts in *Hymns III,* which Fr. Tyson completed in 1979.

In addition to these, an analysis of the approved texts in *The Hymnal 1982* done by Patricia Franz was used by the co-editors. Ms. Franz did this project in partial fulfillment of course requirements in Liturgics while a student at the Anglican School of Theology, Dallas, TX in 1985.

These studies were integrated by Fr. Godwin and Dr. Hatchett working together at the University of the South for two full weeks in the spring of 1985. Assisting them in their work were Barbara Muller, Matthew E. Stockard, Ellen Bradshaw Aitken, Lawrence A. Britt, and Robert C. Schwarz, all of whom were then students at the School of Theology.

It is this Index which formed the basis for Dr. Hatchett's work published in this volume.

Publisher's Preface

This Scriptural Index to *The Hymnal 1982* is a work of great value to all people who work with the hymnody and the Lectionary of the Episcopal Church, whether clergy, musicians, lay readers, or any of a number of other people dedicated to the proclamation of the Word of God. Instead of a simple listing of hymns appropriate to certain scriptural passages, this volume includes exhaustive references to all hymns and portions of hymns which are in any way related to specific scriptural passages. In addition, each entry is charted to show where it appears in the Lectionary of *The Book of Common Prayer*, 1979. This makes the present book a much more flexible and useful resource than such indexes to other hymnals.

The importance of a scriptural index to our hymnody cannot be ignored. When the hymns in a particular service are related to, and expand upon, the readings for the day, the rite will have a unity and integrity which is sure to be impressed upon the congregation. As Dr. Hatchett wrote in his Introduction to *A Liturgical Index to The Hymnal 1982* (Hymnal Studies Five):

One of the most important parts of the planning and preparation for any service is the choice of hymns. Hymns are one of the most vital elements in the participation of the congregation. Hymns set the mood for the rite. Hymns provide a congregational response to lessons and sermons and other important elements in the rites. Hymns are the people's take home package. Because of the musical association people commit hymns to memory more easily and readily than prayers or psalms or other scriptural passages; therefore, the texts of hymns are more likely to recur to people than other texts. People's theology is probably influenced more by the hymns they sing than by the lessons and sermons they hear or the prayers they pray.

It is in the interest of this unity and integrity that *A Scriptural Index to The Hymnal 1982* is published for the Church's use.

A Scriptural Index to The Hymnal 1982

This Index includes scriptural quotations, paraphrases and allusions, and references to significant words, phrases and ideas.

Scriptural citations follow the numeration of the Revised Standard Version of the Bible, except for the psalm citations which follow the Psalter of *The Book of Common Prayer,* 1979.

In the Index, more inclusive references precede more specific ones.

On occasion, attention is called to a particular stanza or stanzas to alert the person using the Index for either one of two reasons: **(1)** a portion of the hymn might in fact serve better than the whole hymn when chosen for the particular propers, especially when a shorter hymn is desirable, as for a sequence, or **(2)**, though a portion of the hymn is related to the particular passage, use of the hymn as a whole might not be appropriate on some occasions for which the passage is appointed.

—Marion J. Hatchett
Sewanee, Tennessee

Genesis

			Daily Office Year One	Daily Office Year Two
1:1—2:3	386, 387	We sing of God, the mighty source		1 Epiphany—Sunday
	398	I sing the almighty power of God		
	405	All things bright and beautiful		
	630	Thanks to God whose Word was spoken		
	651	This is my Father's world		
1:1–17	385	Many and great, O God, are thy works		,, ,,
1:1–5	51	We the Lord's people, heart and voice uniting		,, ,,
1:1–3	371	Thou, whose almighty Word		,, ,,
1:1–2	47	On this day, the first of days		,, ,,
	573	Father eternal, Ruler of creation		
	579	Almighty Father, strong to save		
	608	Eternal Father, strong to save		
1:2	176, 177	Over the chaos of the empty waters		,, ,,
	500	Creator Spirit, by whose aid		
	501, 502	O Holy Spirit, by whose breath		
	506, 507	Praise the Spirit in creation		
1:3–19	389	Let us, with a gladsome mind		,, ,,
1:3–5	8	Morning has broken		,, ,,
	38, 39	Jesus, Redeemer of the world		
	48	O day of radiant gladness		
	52	This day at thy creating word		
1:3–4	27, 28	O blest Creator, source of light		,, ,,
	31, 32	Most holy God, the Lord of heaven		

Lectionary A	Lectionary B	Lectionary C	Pastoral Offices & Episcopal Services	Book of Occasional Services	Lesser Feasts and Fasts
Easter Vigil Trinity Sunday	Easter Vigil	Easter Vigil	Marriage		
,, ,,	,, ,,	,, ,,			
,, ,,	,, ,,	,, ,,			
,, ,,	,, ,,	,, ,,			
,, ,,	,, ,,	,, ,,			
,, ,,	,, ,,	,, ,,			
,, ,,	,, ,,	,, ,,			
,, ,,	,, ,,	,, ,,			
,, ,,	,, ,,	,, ,,			

			Daily Office Year One	Daily Office Year Two
1:3	381	Thy strong word did cleave the darkness		See Above
1:11–18	416	For the beauty of the earth		,, ,,
1:14–19	27, 28 31, 32 38, 39	O blest Creator, source of light Most Holy God, the Lord of heaven Jesus, Redeemer of the world		,, ,,
1:26–27	47	On this day, the first of days		,, ,,
2:4–14	386, 387 398 405 651	We sing of God, the mighty source I sing the almighty power of God All things bright and beautiful This is my Father's world		1 Epiphany—Monday
2:4–9	8	Morning has broken		,, ,,
2:7	47 358	On this day, the first of days Christ the Victorious, give to your servants		,, ,,
2:10	244	Come, pure hearts, in joyful measure (st. 2)		,, ,,
2:24	350 352	O God of love, to thee we bow O God, to those who here profess		,, ,,
3:1–18	60 88 100 270 295	Creator of the stars of night Sing, O sing, this blessed morn (st. 3) Joy to the world! the Lord is come (st. 3) Gabriel's message does away Sing praise to our Creator	Eve of the Annunciation Holy Cross Day—Evening Prayer	4 Advent—Sunday 1 Epiphany—Tuesday Eve of the Annunciation Holy Cross Day—Evening Prayer

Lectionary A	Lectionary B	Lectionary C	Pastoral Offices & Episcopal Services	Book of Occasional Services	Lesser Feasts and Fasts
See Above	See Above	See Above			
,, ,,	,, ,,	,, ,,			
,, ,,	,, ,,	,, ,,			
,, ,,	,, ,,	,, ,,			
1 Lent			Marriage	Advent Festival Christmas Festival	
,, ,,			,, ,,	,, ,,	
,, ,,			,, ,,	,, ,,	
	Proper 22		,, ,,	,, ,,	
,, ,,	Proper 5			Advent Festival Christmas Festival	

			Daily Office Year One	Daily Office Year Two
3:19	358	Christ the Victorious, give to your servants		1 Epiphany—Tuesday
5:24	683, 684	O for a closer walk with God		
11:1–9	230 573	A mighty sound from heaven Father eternal, Ruler of creation		2 Epiphany—Thursday
22:1–14	173	O sorrow deep (st. 2)	Good Friday	4 Epiphany—Wednesday
28:10–22	709	O God of Bethel, by whose hand	St. Bartholomew—Morning Prayer	5 Epiphany—Friday St. Bartholomew—Morning Prayer
28:10–17	453	As Jacob with travel was weary one day	” ”	” ”
28:16	570, 571	All who love and serve your city	” ”	” ”
28:17	360, 361	Only-begotten, Word of God eternal	” ”	” ”
31:42	401	The God of Abraham praise		6 Epiphany—Wednesday
32:22–30	638, 639	Come, O thou Traveler unknown		6 Epiphany—Friday

Lectionary A	Lectionary B	Lectionary C	Pastoral Offices & Episcopal Services	Book of Occasional Services	Lesser Feasts and Fasts
	See Above			See Above	
Pentecost—Early or Vigil Service	Pentecost—Early or Vigil Service	Pentecost—Early or Vigil Service			
Good Friday Easter Vigil	2 Lent Good Friday Easter Vigil	Good Friday Easter Vigil			
St. Michael & All Angels Anniversary of the Dedication of a Church	St. Michael & All Angels Anniversary of the Dedication of a Church	St. Michael & All Angels Anniversary of the Dedication of a Church		Founding of a Church	
,, ,,	,, ,,	,, ,,		,, ,,	
,, ,,	,, ,,	,, ,,		,, ,,	
,, ,,	,, ,,	,, ,,		,, ,,	
		Proper 24			

Exodus:

			Daily Office Year One	Daily Office Year Two
3:6	401	The God of Abraham praise	January 4	4 Lent—Saturday 7 Easter—Sunday
3:13–17	386, 387 401	We sing of God, the mighty source The God of Abraham praise		4 Lent—Saturday 5 Lent—Sunday
3:13–14	439	What wondrous love is this		,, ,,
3:15	718	God of our fathers, whose almighty hand		,, ,,
5:1	648	When Israel was in Egypt's land		5 Lent—Tuesday
6:2–4	393 690	Praise our great and gracious Lord Guide me, O thou great Jehovah		
7:16	648	When Israel was in Egypt's land		5 Lent—Wednesday
8:1, 20	648	When Israel was in Egypt's land		5 Lent—Thursday
9:1, 13	648	When Israel was in Egypt's land		5 Lent—Friday
10:3	648	When Israel was in Egypt's land		
12:1–28	174 202	At the Lamb's high feast we sing The Lamb's high banquet called to share	Easter Day	Easter Day Easter Week—Monday Easter Week—Tuesday

Lectionary A	Lectionary B	Lectionary C	Pastoral Offices & Episcopal Services	Book of Occasional Services	Lesser Feasts and Fasts
	Trinity Sunday	3 Lent			Wulfstan
Of the Holy Trinity	Of the Holy Trinity	3 Lent Of the Holy Trinity			
,, ,,	,, ,,	,, ,,			
,, ,,	,, ,,	,, ,,			
Maundy Thursday	Maundy Thursday	Maundy Thursday			

			Daily Office Year One	Daily Office Year Two
13:21–22	149	Eternal Lord of love, behold your Church		Easter Week—Saturday
	187	Through the Red Sea brought at last		
	363	Ancient of Days, who sittest throned in glory		
	393	Praise our great and gracious Lord		
	522, 523	Glorious things of thee are spoken		
	690	Guide me, O thou great Jehovah		
14:21—15:21	174	At the Lamb's high feast we sing		2 Easter—Sunday
	187	Through the Red Sea brought at last		2 Easter—Monday
	199, 200	Come, ye faithful, raise the strain		2 Easter—Tuesday
	202	The Lamb's high banquet called to share		
	210	The day of resurrection		
	363	Ancient of Days, who sittest throned in glory		
	425	Sing now with joy unto the Lord		
14:22	522, 523	Glorious things of thee are spoken		,, ,,
14:24	149	Eternal Lord of love, behold your Church		,, ,,
	393	Praise our great and gracious Lord		
	690	Guide me, O thou great Jehovah		
15:11	362	Holy, holy, holy! Lord God Almighty		,, ,,
16:4—17:6	307	Lord, enthroned in heavenly splendor		2 Easter—Wednesday
	332	O God, unseen yet ever near		2 Easter—Thursday
	343	Shepherd of souls, refresh and bless		2 Easter—Friday
	522, 523	Glorious things of thee are spoken		2 Easter—Saturday
16:4–35	308, 309	O Food to pilgrims given		,, ,,
	690	Guide me, O thou great Jehovah		

Lectionary A	Lectionary B	Lectionary C	Pastoral Offices & Episcopal Services	Book of Occasional Services	Lesser Feasts and Fasts
Easter Vigil Easter Day—Principal Service	Easter Vigil	Easter Vigil			
,, ,,	,, ,,	,, ,,			
,, ,,	,, ,,	,, ,,			
Easter Day—Principal Service					
	Proper 13			Public Service of Healing	
	,, ,,			,, ,,	

			Daily Office Year One	Daily Office Year Two
17:1–6	**685**	Rock of ages, cleft for me		January 8 2 Easter—Saturday
20:1–20	**56**	O come, O come, Emmanuel		3 Easter—Thursday
23:19	**705**	As those of old their first fruits brought		
33:17–23	**685**	Rock of ages, cleft for me		4 Easter—Wednesday
33:20	**362**	Holy, holy, holy! Lord God Almighty		,, ,,
34:1–35	**56**	O come, O come, Emmanuel		4 Easter—Thursday 4 Easter—Friday
34:28	**143**	The glory of these forty days (st. 2)		

Leviticus:

23:9–14	**705**	As those of old their first fruits brought		5 Easter—Friday

Lectionary A	Lectionary B	Lectionary C	Pastoral Offices & Episcopal Services	Book of Occasional Services	Lesser Feasts and Fasts
3 Lent					3 Lent—Another Proper
	3 Lent				
St. John	St. John	St. John			
,, ,,	,, ,,	,, ,,			
The Transfiguration	The Transfiguration	Last Sunday after the Epiphany The Transfiguration			

Numbers:

			Daily Office Year One	Daily Office Year Two
9:15	**522, 523**	Glorious things of thee are spoken		Proper 6—Monday
20:8–13	**690**	Guide me, O thou great Jehovah		Proper 7—Friday
20:11	**307**	Lord, enthroned in heavenly splendor		,, ,,
	343	Shepherd of souls, refresh and bless		
	522, 523	Glorious things of thee are spoken		
	685	Rock of ages, cleft for me		
24:17	**124**	What star is this, with beams so bright (st. 2)		Proper 8—Saturday
32:32	**393**	Praise our great and gracious Lord		
	690	Guide me, O thou great Jehovah		
34:2	**393**	Praise our great and gracious Lord		
	690	Guide me, O thou great Jehovah		

Deuteronomy:

			Daily Office Year One	Daily Office Year Two
6:5	**551**	Rise up, ye saints of God	Last Epiphany—Sunday	
	581	Where charity and love prevail		
8:3	**343**	Shepherd of souls, refresh and bless	1 Lent—Sunday	January 7
	522, 523	Glorious things of thee are spoken	6 Easter—Monday	
	627	Lamp of our feet, whereby we trace		

Lectionary A	Lectionary B	Lectionary C	Pastoral Offices & Episcopal Services	Book of Occasional Services	Lesser Feasts and Fasts
Holy Name	Holy Name	Holy Name			
For Education	Proper 26 For Education	For Education			
Thanksgiving Day Of the Holy Eucharist	Proper 14 Thanksgiving Day Of the Holy Eucharist	Thanksgiving Day Of the Holy Eucharist		Rogation Procession	

			Daily Office Year One	Daily Office Year Two
26:1–11	**705**	As those of old their first fruits brought	Proper 4—Friday Thanksgiving Day—Morning Prayer	Thanksgiving Day—Morning Prayer
31:6–8	**636, 637**	How firm a foundation, ye saints of the Lord		Proper 9—Friday

Joshua:

			Daily Office Year One	Daily Office Year Two
3:17	**690**	Guide me, O thou great Jehovah		January 4 Proper 10—Thursday
5:6	**624**	Jerusalem the golden		
10:12–14	**18**	As now the sun shines down at noon (*Monday and Thursday*)		Proper 11—Friday
24:3	**393** **690**	Praise our great and gracious Lord Guide me, O thou great Jehovah		Proper 12—Sunday

1 Samuel:

			Daily Office Year One	Daily Office Year Two
2:1–10	**437, 438**	Tell out, my soul, the greatness of the Lord	Proper 6—Tuesday The Presentation—Morning Prayer St. Mary the Virgin—Morning Prayer	4 Advent—Tuesday 6 Easter—Friday The Presentation—Morning Prayer St. Mary the Virgin—Morning Prayer

Lectionary A	Lectionary B	Lectionary C	Pastoral Offices & Episcopal Services	Book of Occasional Services	Lesser Feasts and Fasts
		1 Lent			
	Proper 16				

1 Kings:

			Daily Office Year One	Daily Office Year Two
18:27	**18**	As now the sun shines down at noon (*Tuesday and Saturday*)	Proper 18—Friday	
19:8	**143**	The glory of these forty days (st. 2)	Proper 19—Sunday Eve of the Transfiguration	January 2 Eve of the Transfiguration
19:9–12	**652, 653**	Dear Lord and Father of mankind	,, ,,	January 3 Eve of the Transfiguration
19:11–12	**506, 507**	Praise the Spirit in creation	,, ,,	,, ,,

2 Kings:

2:9–15	**359**	God of the prophets, bless the prophets' heirs	Eve of Ascension Proper 19—Saturday	Eve of Ascension
2:11–12	**143**	The glory of these forty days (st. 2)		

1 Chronicles:

29:14	**291**	We plow the fields, and scatter		

Lectionary A	Lectionary B	Lectionary C	Pastoral Offices & Episcopal Services	Book of Occasional Services	Lesser Feasts and Fasts
	Last Sunday after the Epiphany				
	,, ,,				
	Proper 12	Ascension Day			

2 Chronicles:

			Daily Office Year One	Daily Office Year Two
6:18–21	**518**	Christ is made the sure foundation		
7:1, 12–16	**518**	Christ is made the sure foundation		

Nehemiah:

			Daily Office Year One	Daily Office Year Two
9:19–20	**690**	Guide me, O thou great Jehovah	Proper 27—Monday	
9:19	**149**	Eternal Lord of love, behold your Church	,,	,,
	187	Through the Red Sea brought at last		
	363	Ancient of Days, who sittest throned in glory		
	393	Praise our great and gracious Lord		
	522, 523	Glorious things of thee are spoken		
10:35	**705**	As those of old their first fruits brought		

Job:

			Daily Office Year One	Daily Office Year Two
11:7–9	**476**	Can we by searching find out God		Proper 17—Sunday
33:4	**505**	O Spirit of Life, O Spirit of God		

Lectionary A	Lectionary B	Lectionary C	Pastoral Offices & Episcopal Services	Book of Occasional Services	Lesser Feasts and Fasts
Proper 13					
,, ,,					

			Daily Office Year One	Daily Office Year Two
37:2–5	**569**	God the Omnipotent! King, who ordainest		
38:1–41	**677**	God moves in a mysterious way		Trinity Sunday Proper 18—Saturday Proper 19—Sunday
38:4–7	**426**	Songs of praise the angels sang		,, ,,
38:4	**379**	God is Love, let heaven adore him		,, ,,
38:8–11	**579** **608**	Almighty Father, strong to save Eternal Father, strong to save		,, ,,

Psalms:

			Daily Office Year One and Year Two
16:9	**192**	This joyful Eastertide	1 Advent—Friday Morning Prayer 1 Epiphany—Friday Morning Prayer 8 Epiphany—Friday Morning Prayer 2 Easter—Friday Morning Prayer Proper 2—Friday Morning Prayer Proper 9—Friday Morning Prayer Proper 16—Friday Morning Prayer Proper 23—Friday Morning Prayer

Lectionary A	Lectionary B	Lectionary C	Pastoral Offices & Episcopal Services	Book of Occasional Services	Lesser Feasts and Fasts
For Rogation Days III	Proper 7 For Rogation Days III	For Rogation Days III			
,, ,,	,, ,,	,, ,,			
,, ,,	,, ,,	,, ,,			
,, ,,	,, ,,	,, ,,			

Easter Vigil
Monday in Easter Week
For All Baptized
   Christians
	2 Lent
	Easter Vigil
	Monday in Easter Week
	Proper 16
	Proper 28
	For All Baptized
	   Christians
		Easter Vigil
		Monday in Easter Week
		Proper 8
		For All Baptized
		   Christians
					4 Easter—Sunday
					7 Easter—Thursday
					John of Damascus
					William Laud
					The Martyrs of Japan
					David
					John Donne
					Catherine of Siena
					Justin
					Joseph of Arimathea
					Jeremy Taylor

19	**431**	The stars declare his glory	6 Epiphany—Sunday Evening Prayer 1 Lent—Thursday Evening Prayer 4 Lent—Sunday Evening Prayer 7 Easter—Sunday Evening Prayer Proper 7—Sunday Evening Prayer Proper 14—Sunday Evening Prayer Proper 21—Sunday Evening Prayer Proper 28—Sunday Evening Prayer Holy Innocents—Evening Prayer Conversion of St. Paul—Morning Prayer St. Barnabas—Evening Prayer St. Matthew—Evening Prayer
19:1–6	**362** **409**	Holy, holy, holy! Lord God almighty The spacious firmament on high	,,　　　,,
19:1–4	**434**	Nature with open volume stands	,,　　　,,
21:3–6	**286**	Who are these like stars appearing	1 Advent—Saturday Morning Prayer December 30—Morning Prayer 1 Epiphany—Saturday Morning Prayer 8 Epiphany—Saturday Morning Prayer 2 Easter—Saturday Morning Prayer Proper 2—Saturday Morning Prayer Proper 9—Saturday Morning Prayer Proper 16—Saturday Morning Prayer Proper 23—Saturday Morning Prayer
23	**645, 646** **663** **664** **708**	The King of love my shepherd is The Lord my God my shepherd is My Shepherd will supply my need Savior, like a shepherd lead us	December 30—Evening Prayer 4 Epiphany—Saturday Evening Prayer 2 Lent—Saturday Evening Prayer 5 Easter—Saturday Evening Prayer Proper 5—Saturday Evening Prayer Proper 12—Saturday Evening Prayer Proper 19—Saturday Evening Prayer Proper 26—Saturday Evening Prayer Proper 27—Thursday Evening Prayer St. Thomas—Morning Prayer

Lectionary A	Lectionary B	Lectionary C	Pastoral Offices & Episcopal Services	Book of Occasional Services	Lesser Feasts and Fasts
St. Andrew For a Church Convention	3 Lent Proper 21 St. Andrew For a Church Convention	St. Andrew For a Church Convention		New Year's Eve	1 Lent—Monday Gregory of Nyssa Gregory of Nazianzus Bede the Venerable William Porcher DuBose Bernard Jerome Richard Hooker
,, ,,	,, ,,	,, ,,			,, ,,
,, ,,	,, ,,	,, ,,			,, ,,
					Louis Alfred the Great Edmund of East Anglia (GC 85)
4 Lent 4 Easter Proper 23 Confession of St. Peter Of a Pastor I At Baptism Oppression (GC 82)	4 Easter Convession of St. Peter Of a Pastor I At Baptism Oppression (GC 82)	Confession of St. Peter Of a Pastor I At Baptism Oppression (GC 82)	Thanksgiving for a Child Ministration to the Sick Burial	Baptism of Our Lord Public Service of Healing Burial Consecration of Chrism Special Vocation	5 Lent—Monday Timothy and Titus George Herbert Chad Cuthbert Richard Cyprian Robert Grosseteste Leo the Great

23:4	**344**	Lord, dismiss us with thy blessing	See Above

24:7–10	**65**	Prepare the way, O Zion	4 Advent—Sunday Morning Prayer
	214	Hail the day that sees him rise	4 Epiphany—Sunday Morning Prayer
	436	Lift up your heads, ye mighty gates	2 Lent—Sunday Morning Prayer
			Palm Sunday—Morning Prayer
			5 Easter—Sunday Morning Prayer
			Ascension Day—Evening Prayer
			Proper 5—Sunday Morning Prayer
			Proper 12—Sunday Morning Prayer
			Proper 19—Sunday Morning Prayer
			Proper 26—Sunday Morning Prayer
			The Transfiguration—Morning Prayer

25:3	**703**	Lead us, O Father, in the paths of peace	2 Advent—Monday Morning Prayer
			2 Epiphany—Monday Morning Prayer
			Last Epiphany—Monday Morning Prayer
			3 Easter—Monday Morning Prayer
			Proper 3—Monday Morning Prayer
			Proper 10—Monday Morning Prayer
			Proper 17—Monday Morning Prayer
			Proper 24—Monday Morning Prayer

26:8	**524**	I love thy kingdom, Lord	2 Advent—Tuesday Morning Prayer
			2 Epiphany—Tuesday Morning Prayer
			Last Epiphany—Tuesday Morning Prayer
			3 Easter—Tuesday Morning Prayer
			Proper 3—Tuesday Morning Prayer
			Proper 10—Tuesday Morning Prayer
			Proper 17—Tuesday Morning Prayer
			Proper 24—Tuesday Morning Prayer
			Holy Innocents—Morning Prayer

Lectionary A	Lectionary B	Lectionary C	Pastoral Offices & Episcopal Services	Book of Occasional Services	Lesser Feasts and Fasts
See Above	See Above	See Above	See Above	See Above	See Above
4 Advent				Special Vocation	
Proper 21	1 Lent	Proper 10		Baptism of Our Lord Vigil Before Baptism	3 Lent—Tuesday
Proper 17					John Keble

29:10–11	**569**	God the Omnipotent! King, who ordainest	4 Advent—Sunday Morning Prayer Eve of Epiphany 4 Epiphany—Sunday Morning Prayer 2 Lent—Sunday Morning Prayer Palm Sunday—Morning Prayer 5 Easter—Sunday Morning Prayer Proper 5—Sunday Morning Prayer Proper 12—Sunday Morning Prayer Proper 19—Sunday Morning Prayer Proper 26—Sunday Morning Prayer Anniversary of the Dedication of a Church —Evening Prayer
32:12	**556, 557**	Rejoice, ye pure in heart	2 Advent—Saturday Morning Prayer 2 Epiphany—Saturday Morning Prayer Ash Wednesday—Morning Prayer Last Epiphany—Saturday Morning Prayer 3 Easter—Saturday Morning Prayer Proper 3—Saturday Morning Prayer Proper 10—Saturday Morning Prayer Proper 17—Saturday Morning Prayer Proper 24—Saturday Morning Prayer
33:3	**412**	Earth and all stars	3 Advent—Thursday Evening Prayer January 2—Evening Prayer 6 Epiphany—Saturday Evening Prayer 4 Lent—Saturday Evening Prayer Eve of Pentecost Proper 7—Saturday Evening Prayer Proper 14—Saturday Evening Prayer Proper 21—Saturday Evening Prayer Proper 28—Saturday Evening Prayer St. Matthias—Evening Prayer Independence Day—Morning Prayer St. James—Evening Prayer

Lectionary A	Lectionary B	Lectionary C	Pastoral Offices & Episcopal Services	Book of Occasional Services	Lesser Feasts and Fasts
Proper 14 Of the Holy Trinity	Of the Holy Trinity	Trinity Sunday Of the Holy Trinity			
	7 Epiphany Proper 2	Proper 6 Proper 26			
Easter Vigil	Easter Vigil 6 Easter	Easter Vigil 3 Easter Proper 14		Special Vocation	Ambrose Phillips Brooks Gregory the Great Dunstan The First Book of Common Prayer Ephrem of Edessa Thomas a Kempis Mary and Martha of Bethany John Mason Neale Sergius Consecration of Samuel Seabury Hilda

33:8	**475**	God himself is with us	See Above
36:6	**423**	Immortal, invisible, God only wise	2 Advent—Tuesday Evening Prayer 2 Epiphany—Tuesday Evening Prayer Last Epiphany—Tuesday Evening Prayer 3 Easter—Tuesday Evening Prayer Proper 3—Tuesday Evening Prayer Proper 10—Tuesday Evening Prayer Proper 17—Tuesday Evening Prayer Proper 24—Tuesday Evening Prayer

37	**669**	Commit thou all that grieves thee	2 Advent—Thursday Morning Prayer and
			    Evening Prayer
			2 Epiphany—Thursday Morning Prayer
			    and Evening Prayer
			Last Epiphany—Thursday Morning Prayer
			    and Evening Prayer
			3 Easter—Thursday Morning Prayer and
			    Evening Prayer
			Proper 3—Thursday Morning Prayer and
			    Evening Prayer
			Proper 10—Thursday Morning Prayer and
			    Evening Prayer
			Proper 17—Thursday Morning Prayer and
			    Evening Prayer
			Proper 24—Thursday Morning Prayer and
			    Evening Prayer

39:8	**665**	All my hope on God is founded	2 Advent—Tuesday Evening Prayer 2 Epiphany—Tuesday Evening Prayer Last Epiphany—Tuesday Evening Prayer 3 Easter—Tuesday Evening Prayer Proper 3—Tuesday Evening Prayer Proper 10—Tuesday Evening Prayer Proper 17—Tuesday Evening Prayer Proper 24—Tuesday Evening Prayer

Lectionary A	Lectionary B	Lectionary C	Pastoral Offices & Episcopal Services	Book of Occasional Services	Lesser Feasts and Fasts
See Above	See Above	See Above		See Above	2 Easter—Sunday Gregory the Illuminator
Monday in Holy Week Easter Vigil	Monday in Holy Week Easter Vigil	Monday in Holy Week Easter Vigil		New Year's Eve	Catherine of Siena Mary and Martha of Bethany Aelred (GC 85)
4 Epiphany		7 Epiphany Proper 2 Proper 22			Hilary Thomas Aquinas Anselm Gregory of Nazianzus Alcuin William Porcher DuBose Richard Hooker

42	**658**	As longs the deer for cooling streams	2 Advent—Saturday Evening Prayer 2 Epiphany—Saturday Evening Prayer Last Epiphany—Saturday Evening Prayer 3 Lent—Thursday Morning Prayer 5 Lent—Saturday Evening Prayer 3 Easter—Saturday Evening Prayer Proper 3—Saturday Evening Prayer Proper 10—Saturday Evening Prayer Proper 17—Saturday Evening Prayer Proper 24—Saturday Evening Prayer The Presentation—Morning Prayer
44:1–2	**718**	God of our fathers, whose almighty hand	3 Advent—Monday Evening Prayer 3 Epiphany—Monday Evening Prayer 1 Lent—Monday Evening Prayer 4 Easter—Monday Evening Prayer Proper 4—Monday Evening Prayer Proper 11—Monday Evening Prayer Proper 18—Monday Evening Prayer Proper 25—Monday Evening Prayer
46:1–3	**687, 688**	A mighty fortress is our God	December 24—Morning Prayer December 31—Morning Prayer The Epiphany—Morning Prayer 6 Epiphany—Sunday Evening Prayer 1 Lent—Thursday Evening Prayer 4 Lent—Sunday Evening Prayer 7 Easter—Sunday Evening Prayer Proper 7—Sunday Evening Prayer Proper 14—Sunday Evening Prayer Proper 21—Sunday Evening Prayer Proper 28—Sunday Evening Prayer Eve of Holy Cross Anniversary of the Dedication of a Church —Evening Prayer
46:5	**275**	Hark! the sound of holy voices	,, ,,

Lectionary A	Lectionary B	Lectionary C	Pastoral Offices & Episcopal Services	Book of Occasional Services	Lesser Feasts and Fasts
Easter Vigil St. Mary Magdalene At Baptism	6 Epiphany Easter Vigil Proper 1 St. Mary Magdalene At Baptism	Easter Vigil St. Mary Magdalene At Baptism	Burial	Baptism of Our Lord Vigil Before Baptism	3 Lent—Monday Teresa of Avila (GC 85)
Easter Vigil	Easter Vigil	Easter Vigil Proper 16 Proper 19	Burial	Baptism of Our Lord Vigil Before Baptism	4 Lent—Tuesday
,, ,,	,, ,,	,, ,,	,, ,,	,, ,,	,, ,,

46:10	**578** **607** **613**	O God of love, O King of peace O God of every nation Thy kingdom come, O God	See Above
48:9	**24**	The day thou gavest, Lord, is ended	3 Advent—Tuesday Evening Prayer December 31—Morning Prayer 3 Epiphany—Tuesday Evening Prayer 1 Lent—Tuesday Evening Prayer 4 Easter—Tuesday Evening Prayer Proper 4—Tuesday Evening Prayer Proper 11—Tuesday Evening Prayer Proper 18—Tuesday Evening Prayer Proper 25—Tuesday Evening Prayer The Presentation—Evening Prayer Eve of the Dedication Eves of Apostles and Evangelists
51:1–2	**693** **699**	Just as I am, without one plea Jesus, Lover of my soul	3 Advent—Friday Evening Prayer 3 Epiphany—Friday Evening Prayer 1 Lent—Friday Evening Prayer Holy Week—Monday Morning Prayer 4 Easter—Friday Evening Prayer Proper 4—Friday Evening Prayer Proper 11—Friday Evening Prayer Proper 18—Friday Evening Prayer Proper 25—Friday Evening Prayer
61:8	**11**	Awake, my soul, and with the sun	4 Advent—Monday Morning Prayer 4 Epiphany—Tuesday Morning Prayer 2 Lent—Tuesday Morning Prayer 5 Easter—Tuesday Morning Prayer Proper 5—Tuesday Morning Prayer Proper 12—Tuesday Morning Prayer Proper 19—Tuesday Morning Prayer Proper 26—Tuesday Morning Prayer

Lectionary A	Lectionary B	Lectionary C	Pastoral Offices & Episcopal Services	Book of Occasional Services	Lesser Feasts and Fasts
See Above	See Above	See Above		See Above	
			Consecration of a Church	Founding of a Church	
1 Lent	5 Lent	Proper 19			

66:1	**710**	Make a joyful noise unto the Lord	4 Advent—Tuesday Morning Prayer
			Second Sunday after Christmas—Morning Prayer
			6 Epiphany—Sunday Morning Prayer
			4 Lent—Sunday Morning Prayer
			Easter Week—Monday Evening Prayer
			7 Easter—Sunday Morning Prayer
			Proper 7—Sunday Morning Prayer
			Proper 14—Sunday Morning Prayer
			Proper 21—Sunday Morning Prayer
			Proper 28—Sunday Morning Prayer
			Confession of St. Peter—Morning Prayer
			SS. Peter & Paul—Morning Prayer
			Holy Cross—Morning Prayer
			SS. Simon & Jude—Morning Prayer
67	**538**	God of mercy, God of grace	4 Advent—Tuesday Morning Prayer
			Second Sunday after Christmas—Morning Prayer
			6 Epiphany—Sunday Morning Prayer
			4 Lent—Sunday Morning Prayer
			7 Easter—Sunday Morning Prayer
			Proper 7—Sunday Morning Prayer
			Proper 11—Thursday Morning Prayer
			Proper 14—Sunday Morning Prayer
			Proper 21—Sunday Morning Prayer
			Proper 28—Sunday Morning Prayer
			Confession of St. Peter—Morning Prayer
			St. Mark—Evening Prayer
			St. Barnabas—Morning Prayer
			St. Bartholomew—Evening Prayer
			St. Luke—Evening Prayer
67:2	**539**	O Zion, haste, thy mission high fulfilling	,, ,,

Lectionary A	Lectionary B	Lectionary C	Pastoral Offices & Episcopal Services	Book of Occasional Services	Lesser Feasts and Fasts
5 Easter	5 Easter	Proper 9			3 Easter—Wednesday Augustine of Canterbury
Proper 15 Conversion of St. Paul For the Mission of the Church II	Conversion of St. Paul For the Mission of the Church II	6 Easter Conversion of St. Paul For the Mission of the Church II	Marriage		4 Easter—Wednesday Cornelius the Centurion Jackson Kemper
,, ,,	,, ,,	,, ,,	,, ,,		,, ,,

68:18	**215** **492**	See the Conqueror mounts in triumph Sing, ye faithful, sing with gladness	January 3—Morning Prayer 4 Epiphany—Tuesday Evening Prayer 2 Lent—Tuesday Evening Prayer 5 Easter—Tuesday Evening Prayer Eve of Ascension Proper 5—Tuesday Evening Prayer Proper 12—Tuesday Evening Prayer Proper 19—Tuesday Evening Prayer Proper 26—Tuesday Evening Prayer
71:3	**685**	Rock of ages, cleft for me	4 Epiphany—Thursday Morning Prayer 2 Lent—Thursday Morning Prayer 5 Easter—Thursday Morning Prayer Proper 5—Thursday Morning Prayer Proper 12—Thursday Morning Prayer Proper 19—Thursday Morning Prayer Proper 26—Thursday Morning Prayer
72	**544** **616**	Jesus shall reign where'er the sun Hail to the Lord's Anointed	4 Advent—Wednesday Morning Prayer January 3—Evening Prayer 4 Epiphany—Wednesday Morning Prayer 2 Lent—Wednesday Morning Prayer 5 Easter—Wednesday Morning Prayer Proper 5—Wednesday Morning Prayer Proper 12—Wednesday Morning Prayer Proper 19—Wednesday Morning Prayer Proper 26—Wednesday Morning Prayer The Visitation—Morning Prayer The Transfiguration—Morning Prayer
72:1–8	**65**	Prepare the way, O Zion	,, ,,
81:1	**710**	Make a joyful noise unto the Lord	5 Epiphany—Wednesday Evening Prayer 3 Lent—Wednesday Evening Prayer Proper 6—Wednesday Evening Prayer Proper 13—Wednesday Evening Prayer Proper 20—Wednesday Evening Prayer Proper 27—Wednesday Evening Prayer

Lectionary A	Lectionary B	Lectionary C	Pastoral Offices & Episcopal Services	Book of Occasional Services	Lesser Feasts and Fasts
7 Easter	7 Easter	7 Easter			7 Easter—Tuesday
7 Epiphany Tuesday in Holy Week Proper 2	Tuesday in Holy Week	4 Epiphany Tuesday in Holy Week			Athanasius
2 Advent The Epiphany For Social Justice	The Epiphany For Social Justice	The Epiphany For Social Justice			Frederick Denison Maurice
,, ,,	,, ,,	,, ,,			
	Proper 4				

82:8	**462**	The Lord will come and not be slow	5 Epiphany—Wednesday Evening Prayer 3 Lent—Wednesday Evening Prayer Proper 6—Wednesday Evening Prayer Proper 13—Wednesday Evening Prayer Proper 20—Wednesday Evening Prayer Proper 27—Wednesday Evening Prayer The Nativity of St. John the Baptist— Morning Prayer
84	**517**	How lovely is thy dwelling-place	4 Advent—Sunday Evening Prayer 4 Epiphany—Sunday Evening Prayer 2 Lent—Sunday Evening Prayer 5 Easter—Sunday Evening Prayer Proper 4—Thursday Evening Prayer Proper 5—Sunday Evening Prayer Proper 12—Sunday Evening Prayer Proper 19—Sunday Evening Prayer Proper 26—Sunday Evening Prayer Eve of the Transfiguration Eves of Apostles and Evangelists
85:11, 13	**462**	The Lord will come and not be slow	Christmas Day—Morning Prayer January 4—Morning Prayer 5 Epiphany—Thursday Evening Prayer 3 Lent—Thursday Evening Prayer 6 Easter—Friday Morning Prayer Proper 6—Thursday Evening Prayer Proper 13—Thursday Evening Prayer Proper 20—Thursday Evening Prayer Proper 27—Thursday Evening Prayer Annunciation—Morning Prayer

Lectionary A	Lectionary B	Lectionary C	Pastoral Offices & Episcopal Services	Book of Occasional Services	Lesser Feasts and Fasts
		Proper 15			
Second Sunday after Christmas The Presentation Of a Pastor II At Baptism Anniversary of the Dedication of a Church	Second Sunday after Christmas The Presentation Of a Pastor II At Baptism Anniversary of the Dedication of a Church	Second Sunday after Christmas Proper 25 The Presentation Of a Pastor II At Baptism Anniversary of the Dedication of a Church	Ordination: Deacon Consecration of a Church		Wulfstan Phillips Brooks Chad James DeKoven Richard William Augustus Muhlenberg William White Augustine of Hippo Edward Bouverie Pusey Samuel Isaac Joseph Schereschewsky
Nativity of St. John the Baptist For Peace Human Rights (GC 82)	2 Advent Proper 10 Nativity of St. John the Baptist For Peace Human Rights (GC 82)	3 Advent 4 Epiphany Nativity of St. John the Baptist For Peace Human Rights (GC 82)			Thomas Bray Irenaeus Parents of the Blessed Virgin Mary Aidan Clement of Rome

86:9–10	**462**	The Lord will come and not be slow	5 Epiphany—Thursday Evening Prayer 3 Lent—Thursday Evening Prayer 6 Easter—Friday Morning Prayer Proper 6—Thursday Evening Prayer Proper 13—Thursday Evening Prayer Proper 20—Thursday Evening Prayer Proper 27—Thursday Evening Prayer St. Bartholomew—Morning Prayer
87:1–2	**522, 523**	Glorious things of thee are spoken	January 4—Morning Prayer 5 Epiphany—Saturday Morning Prayer 3 Lent—Saturday Morning Prayer 6 Easter—Saturday Morning Prayer Proper 6—Saturday Morning Prayer Proper 13—Saturday Morning Prayer Proper 20—Saturday Morning Prayer Proper 27—Saturday Morning Prayer The Presentation—Evening Prayer Annunciation—Morning Prayer Eve of Holy Cross
89:9	**579** **608**	Almighty Father, strong to save Eternal Father, strong to save	Christmas Eve—Evening Prayer January 4—Evening Prayer 6 Epiphany—Monday Morning Prayer 4 Lent—Monday Morning Prayer 7 Easter—Monday Morning Prayer Proper 7—Monday Morning Prayer Proper 14—Monday Morning Prayer Proper 21—Monday Morning Prayer Proper 28—Monday Morning Prayer
90:1–5	**680**	O God, our help in ages past	Eve of Holy Name 5 Epiphany—Saturday Morning Prayer 3 Lent—Saturday Morning Prayer 6 Easter—Saturday Morning Prayer Proper 6—Saturday Morning Prayer Proper 13—Saturday Morning Prayer Proper 20—Saturday Morning Prayer Proper 27—Saturday Morning Prayer

Lectionary A	Lectionary B	Lectionary C	Pastoral Offices & Episcopal Services	Book of Occasional Services	Lesser Feasts and Fasts
Proper 11					Saturday after Ash Wednesday
St. Peter & St. Paul	St. Peter & St. Paul	St. Peter & St. Paul			4 Easter—Tuesday Augustine of Hippo
1 Epiphany Proper 8 St. Joseph	1 Epiphany St. Joseph	1 Epiphany St. Joseph		New Year's Eve	
Proper 28 For Labor Day	Proper 23 For Labor Day	For Labor Day	Burial	New Year's Eve Burial	

90:4–7	423	Immortal, invisible, God only wise	See Above
91	375	Give praise and glory unto God	January 11—Evening Prayer 5 Epiphany—Friday Evening Prayer 3 Lent—Friday Evening Prayer 6 Easter—Friday Evening Prayer Proper 6—Friday Evening Prayer Proper 13—Friday Evening Prayer Proper 20—Friday Evening Prayer Proper 27—Friday Evening Prayer
91:1–4	709	O God of Bethel, by whose hand	,,　　　　,,
91:4	43	All praise to thee, my God, this night	,,　　　　,,
95:1–7	399	To God with gladness sing	6 Epiphany—Tuesday Evening Prayer Ash Wednesday—Morning Prayer Last Epiphany—Friday Morning Prayer 1 Lent—Friday Morning Prayer 2 Lent—Friday Morning Prayer 3 Lent—Friday Morning Prayer 4 Lent—Friday Morning Prayer 5 Lent—Friday Morning Prayer Good Friday—Morning Prayer Holy Saturday—Morning Prayer 7 Easter—Tuesday Evening Prayer Proper 7—Tuesday Evening Prayer Proper 14—Tuesday Evening Prayer Proper 21—Tuesday Evening Prayer Proper 28—Tuesday Evening Prayer
95:2	710	Make a joyful noise unto the Lord	,,　　　　,,

Lectionary A	Lectionary B	Lectionary C	Pastoral Offices & Episcopal Services	Book of Occasional Services	Lesser Feasts and Fasts
See Above	See Above	See Above	See Above	See Above	
St. Bartholomew	Proper 24 St. Bartholomew	1 Lent St. Bartholomew	Ministration to the Sick	Public Service of Healing	Antony
,, ,,	,, ,,	,, ,,	,, ,,	,, ,,	,, ,,
,, ,,	,, ,,	,, ,,	,, ,,	,, ,,	,, ,,
3 Lent Proper 29				New Year's Eve	3 Lent—Another Proper 3 Lent—Thursday
,, ,,				,, ,,	

96:1	412	Earth and all stars	4 Advent—Friday Morning Prayer First Sunday after Christmas—Morning Prayer The Epiphany—Evening Prayer 5 Epiphany—Sunday Morning Prayer 3 Lent—Sunday Morning Prayer 6 Easter—Sunday Morning Prayer Ascension Day—Evening Prayer Proper 6—Sunday Morning Prayer Proper 13—Sunday Morning Prayer Proper 18—Thursday Evening Prayer Proper 20—Sunday Morning Prayer Proper 27—Sunday Morning Prayer St. Andrew—Evening Prayer St. Mark—Evening Prayer St. Luke—Evening Prayer The Patronal Feast—Evening Prayer
98	413	New songs of celebration render	3 Advent—Evening Prayer Eve of Epiphany 3 Epiphany—Sunday Morning Prayer 1 Lent—Sunday Morning Prayer Easter Week—Monday Morning Prayer 4 Easter—Sunday Morning Prayer Proper 4—Sunday Morning Prayer Proper 11—Sunday Morning Prayer Proper 18—Sunday Morning Prayer Proper 25—Sunday Morning Prayer St. John—Morning Prayer Nativity of St. John the Baptist—Morning Prayer
98:1	412	Earth and all stars	,, ,,

Lectionary A	Lectionary B	Lectionary C	Pastoral Offices & Episcopal Services	Book of Occasional Services	Lesser Feasts and Fasts
Christmas Day I Proper 24 Of a Missionary I For the Mission of the 　Church I	Christmas Day I Of a Missionary I For the Mission of the 　Church I	Christmas Day I 2 Epiphany Proper 4 Of a Missionary I For the Mission of the 　Church I			4 Easter—Monday 5 Easter—Thursday Channing Moore 　Williams Anskar Cyril and Methodius David Patrick George Augustus Selwyn Jackson Kemper The First Book of 　Common Prayer Dominic Ninian Henry Martyn Willibrord Charles Simeon David Pendleton 　Oakerhater (GC 85)
Christmas Day III Easter Vigil Holy Cross Day Of a Missionary II	Christmas Day III Easter Vigil 3 Easter Holy Cross Day Of a Missionary II	Christmas Day III Easter Vigil Proper 28 Holy Cross Day Of a Missionary II			4 Easter—Saturday 6 Easter—Friday Channing Moore 　Williams Anskar Cyril and Methodius John and Charles Wesley Gregory the Illuminator James Lloyd Breck George Augustus Selwyn Columba Ephrem of Edessa Dominic Henry Martyn Willibrord David Pendleton 　Oakerhater (GC 85)
,, 　 　,,	,, 　 　,,	,, 　 　,,			,, 　 　,,

100	377, 378 391	All people that on earth do dwell Before the Lord's eternal throne	The Epiphany—Evening Prayer January 12 6 Epiphany—Tuesday Morning Prayer 4 Lent—Tuesday Morning Prayer 7 Easter—Tuesday Morning Prayer Proper 7—Tuesday Morning Prayer Proper 14—Tuesday Morning Prayer Proper 21—Tuesday Morning Prayer Proper 28—Tuesday Morning Prayer St. Andrew—Evening Prayer
100:1	710	Make a joyful noise unto the Lord	,, ,,
103	390 410	Praise to the Lord, the Almighty, the King of creation Praise, my soul, the King of Heaven	3 Advent—Sunday Evening Prayer Holy Name—Morning Prayer January 7—Morning Prayer 3 Epiphany—Sunday Evening Prayer 1 Lent—Sunday Evening Prayer Palm Sunday—Evening Prayer Easter Week—Tuesday Morning Prayer 4 Easter—Sunday Evening Prayer Proper 4—Sunday Evening Prayer Proper 11—Sunday Evening Prayer Proper 18—Sunday Evening Prayer Proper 25—Sunday Evening Prayer Proper 25—Thursday Evening Prayer Eve of St. John the Baptist St. Luke—Morning Prayer
103:1–10	411	O bless the Lord, my soul	,, ,,
103:19	535	Ye servants of God, your Master proclaim	,, ,,

Lectionary A	Lectionary B	Lectionary C	Pastoral Offices & Episcopal Services	Book of Occasional Services	Lesser Feasts and Fasts
Proper 6	4 Easter	4 Easter	Ordination: Bishop	Special Vocation	5 Easter—Saturday
,, ,,	,, ,,	,, ,,	,, ,,	,, ,,	,, ,,
Ash Wednesday Proper 19 St. Michael & All Angels Of the Holy Angels For the Departed	8 Epiphany Ash Wednesday Proper 3 St. Michael & All Angels Of the Holy Angels For the Departed	Ash Wednesday 3 Lent St. Michael & All Angels Of the Holy Angels For the Departed	Ministration to the Sick	Rogation Procession All Hallows' Eve Public Service of Healing	2 Lent—Saturday 7 Easter—Friday Clement of Alexandria John and Charles Wesley James DeKoven William Law Dame Julian of Norwich Augustine of Canterbury Remigius
,, ,,	,, ,,	,, ,,	,, ,,	,, ,,	,, ,,
,, ,,	,, ,,	,, ,,	,, ,,	,, ,,	,, ,,

104	**388**	O worship the King, all glorious above	Eve of 1 Epiphany 7 Epiphany—Saturday Evening Prayer Easter Week—Saturday Evening Prayer Eve of Trinity Sunday Proper 1—Saturday Evening Prayer Proper 8—Saturday Evening Prayer Proper 15—Saturday Evening Prayer Proper 22—Saturday Evening Prayer Proper 29—Saturday Evening Prayer St. Michael & All Angels—Evening Prayer
104:5	**379**	God is Love, let heaven adore him	” ”
107:32	**535**	Ye servants of God, your Master proclaim	6 Epiphany—Friday Evening Prayer 4 Lent—Friday Evening Prayer 7 Easter—Friday Evening Prayer Proper 7—Friday Evening Prayer Proper 14—Friday Evening Prayer Proper 21—Friday Evening Prayer Proper 28—Friday Evening Prayer Independence Day—Evening Prayer
108:13	**564, 565**	He who would valiant be	6 Epiphany—Saturday Morning Prayer 4 Lent—Saturday Morning Prayer 7 Easter—Saturday Morning Prayer Proper 7—Saturday Morning Prayer Proper 14—Saturday Morning Prayer Proper 21—Saturday Morning Prayer Proper 28—Saturday Morning Prayer

Lectionary A	Lectionary B	Lectionary C	Pastoral Offices & Episcopal Services	Book of Occasional Services	Lesser Feasts and Fasts
Pentecost For Rogation Days III	Pentecost For Rogation Days III	Pentecost For Rogation Days III		Rogation Procession	
				,, ,,	
	Proper 7				

113:1	535	Ye servants of God, your Master proclaim	1 Advent—Sunday Evening Prayer 4 Advent—Wednesday Evening Prayer January 8—Evening Prayer 1 Epiphany—Sunday Evening Prayer 8 Epiphany—Sunday Evening Prayer Easter Day—Evening Prayer 2 Easter—Sunday Evening Prayer Trinity Sunday—Evening Prayer Proper 9—Sunday Evening Prayer Proper 16—Sunday Evening Prayer Proper 23—Sunday Evening Prayer Eve of the Presentation St. Mary the Virgin—Morning Prayer
113:3	24	The day thou gavest, Lord, is ended	,, ,,
	29, 30	O Trinity of blessed light	
117	380	From all that dwell below the skies	1 Advent—Saturday Evening Prayer 4 Advent—Tuesday Evening Prayer January 8—Morning Prayer 1 Epiphany—Saturday Evening Prayer 8 Epiphany—Saturday Evening Prayer 2 Easter—Saturday Evening Prayer Proper 2—Saturday Evening Prayer Proper 9—Saturday Evening Prayer Proper 16—Saturday Evening Prayer Proper 20—Thursday Morning Prayer Proper 23—Saturday Evening Prayer SS. Simon & Jude—Evening Prayer Eve of the Patronal Feast

Lectionary A	Lectionary B	Lectionary C	Pastoral Offices & Episcopal Services	Book of Occasional Services	Lesser Feasts and Fasts
The Visitation	The Visitation	3 Epiphany Proper 23 The Visitation		All Saints' Day	
,, ,,	,, ,,	,, ,,		,, ,,	
					3 Easter—Friday

118:19–20	**65**	Prepare the way, O Zion	January 8—Morning Prayer 3 Epiphany—Thursday Evening Prayer 7 Epiphany—Sunday Morning Prayer 5 Lent—Sunday Morning Prayer Easter Day—Evening Prayer Easter Week—Friday Evening Prayer Pentecost—Morning Prayer Proper 8—Sunday Morning Prayer Proper 15—Sunday Morning Prayer Proper 22—Sunday Morning Prayer Proper 29—Sunday Morning Prayer St. Stephen—Evening Prayer Confession of St. Peter—Evening Prayer Holy Cross—Evening Prayer
118:24–26	**50**	This is the day the Lord hath made	,, ,,
118:24	**48** **49**	O day of radiant gladness Come, let us with our Lord arise	,, ,,
118:26	**65** **74** **154, 155** **156**	Prepare the way, O Zion Blest be the King whose coming All glory, laud, and honor Ride on! ride on in majesty	,, ,,
119:10	**697**	My God, accept my heart this day	1 Advent—Wednesday Morning Prayer 1 Epiphany—Wednesday Morning Prayer 8 Epiphany—Wednesday Morning Prayer 2 Easter—Wednesday Morning Prayer Proper 2—Wednesday Morning Prayer Proper 9—Wednesday Morning Prayer Proper 16—Wednesday Morning Prayer Proper 23—Wednesday Morning Prayer

Lectionary A	Lectionary B	Lectionary C	Pastoral Offices & Episcopal Services	Book of Occasional Services	Lesser Feasts and Fasts
Palm Sunday Easter Day—Principal Service Easter Day—Evening Service Monday through Saturday in Easter Week 2 Easter	Palm Sunday Easter Day—Principal Service Easter Day—Evening Service Monday through Saturday in Easter Week 2 Easter	Palm Sunday Easter Day—Principal Service Easter Day—Evening Service Monday through Saturday in Easter Week 2 Easter			John of Damascus
,, ,,	,, ,,	,, ,,			
,, ,,	,, ,,	,, ,,			
,, ,,	,, ,,	,, ,,			
6 Epiphany Proper 1	Proper 26				

119:105, 130	**627**	Lamp of our feet, whereby we trace	5 Epiphany—Wednesday Morning Prayer
	632	O Christ, the Word Incarnate	6 Epiphany—Wednesday Morning Prayer
			3 Lent—Wednesday Morning Prayer
			4 Lent—Wednesday Evening Prayer
			6 Easter—Wednesday Morning Prayer
			7 Easter—Wednesday Evening Prayer
			Proper 6—Wednesday Morning Prayer
			Proper 7—Wednesday Evening Prayer
			Proper 13—Wednesday Morning Prayer
			Proper 14—Wednesday Evening Prayer
			Proper 20—Wednesday Morning Prayer
			Proper 21—Wednesday Evening Prayer
			Proper 27—Wednesday Morning Prayer
			Proper 28—Wednesday Evening Prayer
			Conversion of St. Paul—Evening Prayer
121	**668**	I to the hills will lift mine eyes	January 9—Morning Prayer
			7 Epiphany—Tuesday Morning Prayer
			5 Lent—Tuesday Morning Prayer
			Proper 1—Tuesday Morning Prayer
			Proper 8—Tuesday Morning Prayer
			Proper 15—Tuesday Morning Prayer
			Proper 22—Tuesday Morning Prayer
			Proper 29—Tuesday Morning Prayer
			St. Thomas—Morning Prayer
121:3–4	**408**	Sing praise to God who reigns above (st. 2)	” ”
130	**151**	From deepest woe I cry to thee	7 Epiphany—Wednesday Evening Prayer
	666	Out of the depths I call	Ash Wednesday—Evening Prayer
			5 Lent—Wednesday Evening Prayer
			Proper 1—Wednesday Evening Prayer
			Proper 8—Wednesday Evening Prayer
			Proper 15—Wednesday Evening Prayer
			Proper 22—Wednesday Evening Prayer
			Proper 29—Wednesday Evening Prayer

Lectionary A	Lectionary B	Lectionary C	Pastoral Offices & Episcopal Services	Book of Occasional Services	Lesser Feasts and Fasts
Proper 12					
		Proper 24	Burial	Public Service of Healing Burial	Polycarp John Coleridge Patteson Francis of Assisi
		,, ,,	,, ,,	,, ,,	,, ,,

5 Lent
Holy Saturday
Pentecost—Vigil or Early
  Service
For the Departed
	3 Epiphany
	Holy Saturday
	Pentecost—Vigil or Early
	  Service
	Proper 5
	For the Departed
		Holy Saturday
		Pentecost—Vigil or Early
		  Service
		For the Departed
			Burial	New Year's Eve
				All Hallows' Eve
				Public Service of Healing
				Burial
					1 Lent—Friday
					All Faithful Departed

131	**670**	Lord, for ever at thy side	January 9—Evening Prayer 7 Epiphany—Thursday Morning Prayer 5 Lent—Thursday Morning Prayer Proper 1—Thursday Morning Prayer Proper 8—Thursday Morning Prayer Proper 15—Thursday Morning Prayer Proper 22—Thursday Morning Prayer Proper 29—Thursday Morning Prayer
136:1–9, 25–26	**389**	Let us, with a gladsome mind	5 Epiphany—Saturday Evening Prayer 3 Lent—Saturday Evening Prayer Easter Week—Friday Morning Prayer 6 Easter—Saturday Evening Prayer Proper 6—Saturday Evening Prayer Proper 13—Saturday Evening Prayer Proper 20—Saturday Evening Prayer Proper 27—Saturday Evening Prayer
139:1–11	**702**	Lord, thou hast searched me and dost know	3 Advent—Saturday Evening Prayer January 10—Morning Prayer 3 Epiphany—Saturday Evening Prayer 1 Lent—Saturday Evening Prayer 4 Easter—Saturday Evening Prayer Proper 4—Saturday Evening Prayer Proper 11—Saturday Evening Prayer Proper 18—Saturday Evening Prayer Proper 25—Saturday Evening Prayer SS. Philip & James—Evening Prayer
144:9	**412**	Earth and all stars	7 Epiphany—Saturday Morning Prayer 5 Lent—Saturday Morning Prayer Proper 1—Saturday Morning Prayer Proper 8—Saturday Morning Prayer Proper 15—Saturday Morning Prayer Proper 22—Saturday Morning Prayer Proper 29—Saturday Morning Prayer

Lectionary A	Lectionary B	Lectionary C	Pastoral Offices & Episcopal Services	Book of Occasional Services	Lesser Feasts and Fasts
Easter Day—Evening Service	Easter Day—Evening Service	Easter Day—Evening Service			
3 Epiphany Of the Holy Spirit At Confirmation	Of the Holy Spirit At Confirmation	Of the Holy Spirit At Confirmation	Burial	Public Service of Healing	Anselm Basil the Great Jeremy Taylor Bernard Teresa of Avila (GC 85)

145	**404**	We will extol you, ever-blessed Lord	Second Sunday after Christmas—Evening Prayer 7 Epiphany—Sunday Evening Prayer 5 Lent—Sunday Evening Prayer Easter Week—Saturday Morning Prayer Pentecost—Evening Prayer Proper 8—Sunday Evening Prayer Proper 13—Thursday Morning Prayer Proper 15—Sunday Evening Prayer Proper 22—Sunday Evening Prayer Proper 29—Sunday Evening Prayer St. John—Evening Prayer St. Mark—Morning Prayer Thanksgiving Day—Evening Prayer
145:1–12	**414**	God, my King, thy might confessing	,, ,,
145:13	**24**	The day thou gavest, Lord, is ended	,, ,,
146	**429**	I'll praise my Maker while I've breath	1 Advent—Sunday Morning Prayer 4 Advent—Thursday Evening Prayer 1 Epiphany—Sunday Morning Prayer 5 Epiphany—Thursday Morning Prayer 8 Epiphany—Sunday Morning Prayer Easter Week—Thursday Morning Prayer 2 Easter—Sunday Morning Prayer Trinity Sunday—Morning Prayer Proper 9—Sunday Morning Prayer Proper 16—Sunday Morning Prayer Proper 23—Sunday Morning Prayer The Visitation—Evening Prayer St. Barnabas—Evening Prayer

Lectionary A	Lectionary B	Lectionary C	Pastoral Offices & Episcopal Services	Book of Occasional Services	Lesser Feasts and Fasts
Proper 9 Proper 20 Independence Day	Independence Day	5 Easter Independence Day	Ministration to the Sick	Public Service of Healing	4 Lent—Wednesday 5 Easter—Monday Nicholas Thomas Ken Frederick Denison Maurice James Lloyd Breck Irenaeus William Reed Huntington Charles Simeon Aelred (GC 85)
,, ,,	,, ,,	,, ,,		,, ,,	,, ,,
,, ,,	,, ,,	,, ,,		,, ,,	,, ,,
3 Advent For Social Service World Hunger (GC 82)	Proper 18 Proper 27 For Social Service World Hunger (GC 82)	Proper 21 For Social Service World Hunger (GC 82)	New Ministry	Public Service of Healing	2 Easter—Monday Wulfstan William Wilberforce Margaret Elizabeth

148	373	Praise the Lord! ye heavens adore him	2 Advent—Sunday Morning Prayer
	394, 395	Creating God, your fingers trace	4 Advent—Friday Evening Prayer
	400	All creatures of our God and King	Holy Name—Evening Prayer
	406, 407	Most high, omnipotent, good Lord	January 11—Morning Prayer
	412	Earth and all stars (st. 2)	2 Epiphany—Sunday Morning Prayer
	432	O praise ye the Lord! Praise him in the height	Last Epiphany—Sunday Morning Prayer
			Easter Day—Morning Prayer
			Easter Week—Thursday Evening Prayer
			3 Easter—Sunday Morning Prayer
			Proper 3—Sunday Morning Prayer
			Proper 10—Sunday Morning Prayer
			Proper 17—Sunday Morning Prayer
			Proper 24—Sunday Morning Prayer
			St. Michael & All Angels—Morning Prayer
			All Saints' Day—Evening Prayer
			The Patronal Feast—Morning Prayer
148:1–2	618	Ye watchers and ye holy ones	" "
	619	Sing alleluia forth in duteous praise	
150	390	Praise to the Lord, the Almighty, the King of creation	2 Advent—Sunday Morning Prayer
	412	Earth and all stars (st. 3)	4 Advent—Friday Evening Prayer
	420	When in our music God is glorified	January 11—Morning Prayer
	430	Come, O come, our voices raise	2 Epiphany—Sunday Morning Prayer
	432	O praise ye the Lord! Praise him in the height	Last Epiphany—Sunday Morning Prayer
			Easter Day—Morning Prayer
			3 Easter—Sunday Morning Prayer
			Proper 3—Sunday Morning Prayer
			Proper 10—Sunday Morning Prayer
			Proper 17—Sunday Morning Prayer
			Proper 24—Sunday Morning Prayer
			St. Michael & All Angels—Evening Prayer
			All Saints' Day—Evening Prayer
			Eves of Apostles and Evangelists

Lectionary A	Lectionary B	Lectionary C	Pastoral Offices & Episcopal Services	Book of Occasional Services	Lesser Feasts and Fasts
6 Easter Of the Holy Angels	Of the Holy Angels	Of the Holy Angels		New Year's Eve	6 Easter—Wednesday Francis of Assisi
,, ,,	,, ,,	,, ,,		,, ,,	,, ,,
Trinity Sunday					

Proverbs:

			Daily Office Year One	Daily Office Year Two
8:1–31	**56**	O come, O come, Emmanuel	St. John—Morning Prayer	St. John—Morning Prayer 7 Epiphany—Friday 7 Epiphany—Saturday Proper 2—Friday Proper 2—Saturday
8:29	**379**	God is Love, let heaven adore him	,, ,,	,, ,,

Song of Solomon:

2:10–13	**213**	Come away to the skies		

Isaiah:

1:18	**693** **699**	Just as I am, without one plea Jesus, Lover of my soul	1 Advent—Monday	
2:4	**542** **613**	Christ is the world's true Light Thy kingdom come, O God	1 Advent—Wednesday	
4:5–6	**522, 523**	Glorious things of thee are spoken	1 Advent—Saturday SS. Simon & Jude—Evening Prayer	7 Easter—Wednesday SS. Simon & Jude—Evening Prayer

Lectionary A	Lectionary B	Lectionary C	Pastoral Offices & Episcopal Services	Book of Occasional Services	Lesser Feasts and Fasts
			Marriage		Agnes Clare
		Proper 26			2 Lent—Tuesday

1 Advent
For the Mission of the
  Church I
	For the Mission of the
	  Church I
		For the Mission of the
		  Church I			

Easter Vigil	Easter Vigil	Easter Vigil			

			Daily Office Year One	Daily Office Year Two
6:1–7	**362**	Holy, holy, holy! Lord God Almighty	2 Advent—Wednesday	
6:1–3	**324**	Let all mortal flesh keep silence	,, ,,	
	364	O God, we praise thee, and confess		
	366	Holy God, we praise thy Name		
	367	Round the Lord in glory seated		
	401	The God of Abraham praise		
	643	My God, how wonderful thou art		
6:3	**48**	O day of radiant gladness	,, ,,	
7:14	**56**	O come, O come, Emmanuel	2 Advent—Friday	
	87	Hark! the herald angels sing (st. 2)		
	88	Sing, O sing, this blessed morn (st. 3)		
	496, 497	How bright appears the Morning Star		
9:2–7	**91**	Break forth, O beauteous heavenly light	3 Advent—Tuesday	
	125, 126	The people who in darkness walked		
	381	Thy strong word did cleave the darkness		
9:2	**6**	Christ, whose glory fills the skies	,, ,,	
9:6	**88**	Sing, O sing, this blessed morn (st. 1)	,, ,,	
	542	Christ is the world's true Light		
	640	Watchman, tell us of the night		
11:1–10	**56**	O come, O come, Emmanuel	4 Advent—Monday	Eve of the Visitation
	81	Lo, how a Rose e'er blooming	Day of Pentecost	
	307	Lord, enthroned in heavenly splendor	Eve of the Visitation	
	496, 497	How bright appears the Morning Star		

Lectionary A	Lectionary B	Lectionary C	Pastoral Offices & Episcopal Services	Book of Occasional Services	Lesser Feasts and Fasts
		Trinity Sunday	Ordination: Priest	Advent Festival	
		,, ,,	,, ,,	,, ,,	
		,, ,,	,, ,,	,, ,,	
4 Advent The Annunciation	The Annunciation	The Annunciation		Advent Festival Christmas Festival	
Christmas Day I	Christmas Day I	Christmas Day I			
,, ,,	,, ,,	,, ,,			
,, ,,	,, ,,	,, ,,			
2 Advent Of the Incarnation	Of the Incarnation	Of the Incarnation		Advent Festival Public Service of Healing	

			Daily Office Year One	Daily Office Year Two
11:2	**226, 227** **500** **501, 502**	Come, thou Holy Spirit bright Creator Spirit, by whose aid O Holy Spirit, by whose breath	See Above	See Above
11:6–9	**597**	O day of peace that dimly shines	,, ,,	,, ,,
11:9	**503, 504** **534**	Come, Holy Ghost, our souls inspire God is working his purpose out	,, ,,	,, ,,
12:2–6	**678, 679**	Surely it is God who saves me	December 29	
12:4–5	**493**	O for a thousand tongues to sing	,, ,,	
21:11–12	**640**	Watchman, tell us of the night		
22:22	**56**	O come, O come, Emmanuel		
26:4	**635**	If thou but trust in God to guide thee	December 31	
28:16	**518** **525**	Christ is made the sure foundation The Church's one foundation	4 Advent—Wednesday SS. Simon & Jude—Morning Prayer	SS. Simon & Jude—Morning Prayer
29:18–19	**493**	O for a thousand tongues to sing	4 Advent—Thursday	
30:15	**652, 653**	Dear Lord and Father of mankind		
32:2	**498**	Beneath the cross of Jesus		
33:20–21	**522, 523**	Glorious things of thee are spoken	4 Advent—Friday	

Lectionary A	Lectionary B	Lectionary C	Pastoral Offices & Episcopal Services	Book of Occasional Services	Lesser Feasts and Fasts
See Above	See Above	See Above		See Above	
,, ,,	,, ,,	,, ,,		,, ,,	
,, ,,	,, ,,	,, ,,		,, ,,	
For the Nation	2 Easter For the Nation	Proper 16 For the Nation			

			Daily Office Year One	Daily Office Year Two
35:5–6	**493**	O for a thousand tongues to sing (st. 5)	December 24	
35:10	**392** **624**	Come, we that love the Lord Jerusalem the golden	December 24	
40:1–11	**75**	There's a voice in the wilderness crying	1 Epiphany—Sunday	
40:1–5	**59** **65** **67** **70** **76**	Hark! a thrilling voice is sounding Prepare the way, O Zion Comfort, comfort ye my people Herald, sound the note of judgment On Jordan's bank the Baptist's cry	,, ,,	
40:9	**99**	Go tell it on the mountain (Refrain)	,, ,,	
40:11	**478** **708**	Jesus, our mighty Lord Savior, like a shepherd lead us	,, ,,	
41:10–11	**636, 637**	How firm a foundation, ye saints of the Lord	1 Epiphany—Wednesday	
43:2	**636, 637**	How firm a foundation, ye saints of the Lord	1 Epiphany—Saturday	
45:23	**60** **252** **435**	Creator of the stars of night Jesus! Name of wondrous love At the Name of Jesus	2 Epiphany—Friday Conversion of St. Paul—Morning Prayer	Conversion of St. Paul—Morning Prayer

Lectionary A	Lectionary B	Lectionary C	Pastoral Offices & Episcopal Services	Book of Occasional Services	Lesser Feasts and Fasts
3 Advent For the Unity of the Church	Proper 18 For the Unity of the Church	For the Unity of the Church		Advent Festival Christmas Festival	
,, ,,	For the Unity of the Church	,, ,,		,, ,,	
Nativity of St. John the Baptist	2 Advent Nativity of St. John the Baptist	Nativity of St. John the Baptist		Advent Festival Christmas Festival	
,, ,,	,, ,,	,, ,,		,, ,,	
,, ,,	,, ,,	,, ,,		,, ,,	
,, ,,	,, ,,	,, ,,		,, ,,	
3 Easter					
Palm Sunday Holy Cross Day	Palm Sunday Holy Cross Day	Palm Sunday Holy Cross Day			

			Daily Office Year One	Daily Office Year Two
50:6	**168, 169**	O sacred head, sore wounded	3 Epiphany—Friday	
51:12–16	**379**	God is Love, let heaven adore him	4 Epiphany—Sunday	
51:13–16	**580**	God, who stretched the spangled heavens		
52:1–8	**61, 62**	"Sleepers, wake!" A voice astounds us	Epiphany January 7 4 Epiphany—Tuesday Annunciation—Morning Prayer St. Luke—Evening Prayer The Patronal Feast—Morning Prayer Eves of Apostles and Evangelists	Annunciation—Morning Prayer St. Luke—Evening Prayer The Patronal Feast—Morning Prayer Eves of Apostles and Evangelists
52:7	**539**	O Zion, haste, thy mission high fulfilling	,, ,,	,, ,,
52:8–10	**540** **640**	Awake, thou Spirit of the watchmen Watchman, tell us of the night	,, ,,	,, ,,
52:13—53:12	**458**	My song is love unknown		
53:1–12	**158** **168, 169**	Ah, holy Jesus, how hast thou offended O sacred head, sore wounded		
53:5	**208**	The strife is o'er, the battle done		
55:12–13	**100**	Joy to the world! the Lord is come	4 Epiphany—Thursday	

Lectionary A	Lectionary B	Lectionary C	Pastoral Offices & Episcopal Services	Book of Occasional Services	Lesser Feasts and Fasts
Wednesday in Holy Week	Wednesday in Holy Week Proper 19	Wednesday in Holy Week			
Christmas Day III St. Mark Of a Missionary I	Christmas Day III St. Mark Of a Missionary I	Christmas Day III St. Mark Of a Missionary			Thomas Bray David Pendleton Oakerhater (GC 85)
,, ,,	,, ,,	,, ,,			,, ,,
,, ,,	,, ,,	,, ,,			,, ,,
Palm Sunday Good Friday Of the Holy Cross	Palm Sunday Good Friday Of the Holy Cross	Palm Sunday Good Friday Of the Holy Cross		Public Service of Healing	
,, ,,	,, ,,	,, ,,		,, ,,	
,, ,,	,, ,,	,, ,,		,, ,,	
Proper 10 For a Church Convention	For a Church Convention	For a Church Convention			

			Daily Office Year One	Daily Office Year Two
56:6–7	**51**	We the Lord's people, heart and voice uniting	4 Epiphany—Friday	
57:15	**643**	My God, how wonderful thou art	5 Epiphany—Sunday	
58:5–10	**145**	Now quit your care	5 Epiphany—Monday	
60:1–22	**543**	O Zion, tune thy voice	5 Epiphany—Thursday	
60:2	**672**	O very God of very God	,, ,,	
60:19–20	**119**	As with gladness men of old (sts. 4–5)		
61:1–2	**71, 72**	Hark! the glad sound! the Savior comes	Eve of 1 Epiphany 5 Epiphany—Friday	Eve of 1 Epiphany
61:1	**539**	O Zion, haste, thy mission high fulfilling	,, ,,	
62:3	**450, 451**	All hail the power of Jesus' Name	5 Epiphany—Saturday	Holy Name
65:17–19	**620** **624**	Jerusalem, my happy home Jerusalem the golden	Eve of Holy Name 6 Epiphany—Friday Proper 1—Thursday Proper 28—Saturday St. James of Jerusalem—Evening	Eve of Holy Name St. James of Jerusalem—Evening

Lectionary A	Lectionary B	Lectionary C	Pastoral Offices & Episcopal Services	Book of Occasional Services	Lesser Feasts and Fasts
Proper 15					
		Proper 11			
Ash Wednesday World Hunger (GC 82)	Ash Wednesday World Hunger (GC 82)	Ash Wednesday World Hunger (GC 82)			Friday after Ash Wednesday Saturday after Ash Wednesday Martin of Tours
The Epiphany	The Epiphany	The Epiphany			
,, ,,	,, ,,	,, ,,			
Of the Holy Spirit At Confirmation	Of the Holy Spirit At Confirmation	Of the Holy Spirit At Confirmation	Burial Ordination: Burial	Baptism of Our Lord Public Service of Healing Consecration of Chrism	Absalom Jones
,, ,,	,, ,,	,, ,,	,, ,,	,, ,,	,, ,,
1 Christmas	1 Christmas	1 Christmas 2 Epiphany			
	3 Advent			Advent Festival	4 Lent—Monday

			Daily Office Year One	Daily Office Year Two
65:17	296	We know that Christ is raised and dies no more	See Above	

Jeremiah:

			Daily Office Year One	Daily Office Year Two
8:22	231, 232 676	By all your saints still striving (Saint Luke) There is a balm in Gilead	3 Lent—Wednesday	
10:23	703	Lead us O Father, in the paths of peace	3 Lent—Thursday	
31:6	61, 62	"Sleepers, wake!" A voice astounds us	St. Mary the Virgin—Evening Prayer	St. Mary the Virgin—Evening Prayer

Lamentations:

			Daily Office Year One	Daily Office Year Two
1:12	164 458	Alone thou goest forth, O Lord My song is love unknown	Proper 24—Tuesday	Holy Week—Monday
3:22–23	10	New every morning is the love		Good Friday
5:19	24	The day thou gavest, Lord, is ended		

Lectionary A	Lectionary B	Lectionary C	Pastoral Offices & Episcopal Services	Book of Occasional Services	Lesser Feasts and Fasts
	See Above			See Above	See Above
	Proper 6				
			Burial		

Ezekiel:

			Daily Office Year One	Daily Office Year Two
1:4–28	**235**	Come sing, ye choirs exultant (st. 2)	Ascension Day	
10:9–22	**235**	Come sing, ye choirs exultant (st. 2)		
34:1–31	**478**	Jesus, our mighty Lord	7 Easter—Friday Confession of St. Peter—Evening Prayer	Proper 1—Wednesday Confession of St. Peter—Evening Prayer

Daniel:

			Daily Office Year One	Daily Office Year Two
7:9–14	**363**	Ancient of Days, who sittest throned in glory	The Transfiguration—Evening Prayer	Ascension Day The Transfiguration—Evening Prayer
	365	Come, thou almighty King		
	401	The God of Abraham praise		
	423	Immortal, invisible, God only wise		
7:13–14	**57, 58**	Lo! he comes, with clouds descending		
	454	Jesus came, adored by angels		
8:15–17	**282, 283**	Christ, the fair glory of the holy angels (st. 3)		
9:3	**143**	The glory of these forty days (st. 3)		1 Lent—Sunday
9:20–23	**282, 283**	Christ, the fair glory of the holy angels (st. 3)		

Lectionary A	Lectionary B	Lectionary C	Pastoral Offices & Episcopal Services	Book of Occasional Services	Lesser Feasts and Fasts
	Ascension Day				
Proper 29 St. Peter & St. Paul Of a Pastor I	4 Easter St. Peter & St. Paul Of a Pastor I	St. Peter & St. Paul Of a Pastor I		Rogation Procession	
Ascension Day Of the Holy Angels Of the Reign of Christ	Proper 29 Of the Holy Angels Of the Reign of Christ	Of the Holy Angels Of the Reign of Christ			
,,　　　,,	,,　　　,,	,,　　　,,			
					2 Lent—Monday

			Daily Office Year One	Daily Office Year Two
10:10–21	282, 283	Christ, the fair glory of the holy angels (st. 2)		
12:1–4	282, 283	Christ, the fair glory of the holy angels (st. 2)	Easter Week—Friday St. Michael and All Angels—Evening Prayer	St. Michael and All Angels—Evening Prayer

Hosea:

13:14	188, 189	Love's redeeming work is done		Proper 22—Sunday

Joel:

3:10	542	Christ is the world's true Light	Proper 29—Monday	Proper 27—Saturday

Micah:

4:3	542 613	Christ is the world's true Light Thy Kingdom come, O God	Independence Day—Evening Prayer	Christmas Day Proper 22—Friday Independence Day—Evening Prayer

Lectionary A	Lectionary B	Lectionary C	Pastoral Offices & Episcopal Services	Book of Occasional Services	Lesser Feasts and Fasts
Easter Day—Evening Service	Easter Day—Evening Service Proper 28	Easter Day—Evening Service			
For Peace	3 Easter For Peace	For Peace			

			Daily Office Year One	Daily Office Year Two
6:6–8	605	What does the Lord require		Proper 23—Sunday

Habukkuk:

2:14	534	God is working his purpose out		Proper 28—Monday
2:20	324 475	Let all mortal flesh keep silence God himself is with us		,, ,,
3:17–18	667	Sometimes a light surprises (st. 4)		Last Epiphany—Thursday Proper 28—Tuesday

Haggai:

2:7	56	O come, O come, Emmanuel	Proper 25—Sunday The Presentation—Evening Prayer Eve of the Dedication	2 Advent—Saturday The Presentation—Evening Prayer Eve of the Dedication

Lectionary A	Lectionary B	Lectionary C	Pastoral Offices & Episcopal Services	Book of Occasional Services	Lesser Feasts and Fasts
4 Epiphany Of a Saint I	Of a Saint I	Of a Saint I			
5 Epiphany					

Zechariah:

			Daily Office Year One	Daily Office Year Two
2:13	324	Let all mortal flesh keep silence	Christmas Day The Visitation—Evening Prayer St. Mary the Virgin—Evening Prayer	3 Advent—Tuesday The Visitation—Evening Prayer St. Mary the Virgin—Evening Prayer
9:9	156	Ride on! ride on in majesty	Palm Sunday	Palm Sunday Proper 29—Sunday
13:1	686 699	Come, thou fount of every blessing Jesus, Lover of my soul		Proper 29—Thursday

Malachi:

			Daily Office Year One	Daily Office Year Two
3:1	65 67 70 75 76 93 657	Prepare the way, O Zion Comfort, comfort ye my people Herald, sound the note of judgment There's a voice in the wilderness crying On Jordan's bank the Baptist's cry Angels, from the realms of glory (st. 4) Love divine, all loves excelling	Nativity of St. John the Baptist— Morning Prayer	Proper 28—Friday Nativity of St. John the Baptist— Morning Prayer
4:2	6, 7 87 371 490 596 667 672	Christ, whose glory fills the skies Hark! the herald angels sing (st. 3) Thou, whose almighty Word I want to walk as a child of the light Judge eternal, throned in splendor Sometimes a light surprises O very God of very God	Nativity of St. John the Baptist— Evening Prayer	Proper 28—Saturday Nativity of St. John the Baptist— Evening Prayer

Lectionary A	Lectionary B	Lectionary C	Pastoral Offices & Episcopal Services	Book of Occasional Services	Lesser Feasts and Fasts
Proper 9					
The Presentation	The Presentation	The Presentation			
		Proper 28			

Tobit:

			Daily Office Year One	Daily Office Year Two
3:16—12:15	282, 283	Christ, the fair glory of the holy angels (st. 4)		

Wisdom:

			Daily Office Year One	Daily Office Year Two
7:22	56	O come, O come Emmanuel	5 Easter—Sunday	
10:18–19	174	At the Lamb's high feast we sing	5 Easter—Tuesday	
	187	Through the Red Sea brought at last		
	199, 200	Come, ye faithful, raise the strain		
	202	The Lamb's high banquet called to share		
	210	The day of resurrection		
10:18	363	Ancient of Days, who sittest throned in glory		

Ecclesiasticus:

			Daily Office Year One	Daily Office Year Two
44:1–14	289	Our Father, by whose servants		Proper 26—Thursday
50:22–24	396, 397	Now thank we all our God		Proper 26—Friday

Lectionary A	Lectionary B	Lectionary C	Pastoral Offices & Episcopal Services	Book of Occasional Services	Lesser Feasts and Fasts
			Marriage		Elizabeth
					Bede the Venerable
All Saints' Day	All Saints' Day	All Saints' Day		All Saints' Day	Dunstan
Proper 26—Friday					

2 Esdras:

			Daily Office Year One	Daily Office Year Two
2:34–35	358	Christ the Victorious, give to your servants		
2:42–48	286	Who are these like stars appearing	All Saints' Day—Morning Prayer	All Saints' Day—Morning Prayer

Song of the Three Young Men:

35–65	400	All creatures of our God and King		
	406, 407	Most High, omnipotent, good Lord		
	428	O all ye works of God, now come		

Matthew:

			Daily Office Year One	Daily Office Year Two
1:18–25	54	Savior of the nations, come	First Sunday after Christmas	December 24
	55	Redeemer of the nations, come	St. Matthias—Morning Prayer	Holy Name
	81	Lo, how a Rose e'er blooming		St. Matthias—Morning Prayer
	231, 232	By all your saints still striving (Saint Joseph)		
	248, 249	To the Name of our salvation		
	250	Now greet the swiftly changing year (st. 2)		
	252	Jesus! Name of wondrous love		
	260	Come now, and praise the humble saint		
	261, 262	By the Creator, Joseph was appointed		
1:21–23	435	At the Name of Jesus	" "	" "

Lectionary A	Lectionary B	Lectionary C	Pastoral Offices & Episcopal Services	Book of Occasional Services	Lesser Feasts and Fasts
Of a Martyr I	Of a Martyr I	Of a Martyr I			
4 Advent					
,, ,,					

			Daily Office Year One	Daily Office Year Two
1:22–23	**56**	O come, O come, Emmanuel	See Above	See Above
1:23	**265**	The angel Gabriel from heaven came	,, ,,	,, ,,
	475	God himself is with us		
	496, 497	How bright appears the Morning Star		
2:1–12	**92**	On this day earth shall ring (st. 3)	Proper 18—Wednesday	
	93	Angels, from the realms of glory (st. 3)		
	109	The first Nowell the angel did say		
	112	In the bleak midwinter (st. 4)		
	114	'Twas in the moon of wintertime (sts. 3 & 4)		
	115	What child is this, who, laid to rest		
	117, 118	Brightest and best of the stars of the morning		
	119	As with gladness men of old		
	124	What star is this, with beams so bright		
	127	Earth has many a noble city		
	128	We three kings of Orient are		
	131, 132	When Christ's appearing was made known (sts. 1 & 2)		
	135	Songs of thankfulness and praise (st. 1)		
	491	Where is this stupendous stranger		
2:1	**307**	Lord, enthroned in heavenly splendor	,, ,,	
	452	Glorious the day when Christ was born		
2:13–23	**231, 232**	By all your saints still striving (Saint Joseph)	Proper 18—Thursday	
	260	Come now, and praise the humble saint		
	261, 262	By the Creator, Joseph was appointed		
2:13–18	**98**	Unto us a boy is born (st. 3)	,, ,,	
	113	Oh, sleep now, holy baby		

Lectionary A	Lectionary B	Lectionary C	Pastoral Offices & Episcopal Services	Book of Occasional Services	Lesser Feasts and Fasts
See Above					
,, ,,					
2 Christmas The Epiphany	2 Christmas The Epiphany	2 Christmas The Epiphany			
,, ,,	,, ,,	,, ,,			
2 Christmas Holy Innocents	2 Christmas Holy Innocents	2 Christmas Holy Innocents			
,, ,,	,, ,,	,, ,,			

			Daily Office Year One	Daily Office Year Two
2:16–18	231, 232	By all your saints still striving (The Holy Innocents)	See Above	
	246	In Bethlehem a newborn boy		
	247	Lully, lullay, thou little tiny child		
3:1–12	59	Hark! a thrilling voice is sounding	3 Advent—Thursday	3 Easter—Monday
	69	What is the crying at Jordan	Proper 18—Friday	3 Easter—Tuesday
	70	Herald, sound the note of judgment		
	76	On Jordan's bank the Baptist's cry		
3:1–3	67	Comfort, comfort ye my people	,, ,,	,, ,,
	75	There's a voice in the wilderness crying		
3:3	65	Prepare the way, O Zion	,, ,,	,, ,,
3:4	143	The glory of these forty days (st. 3)	,, ,,	,, ,,
3:11	500	Creator Spirit, by whose aid	,, ,,	,, ,,
	501, 502	O Holy Spirit, by whose breath		
	503, 504	Come, Holy Ghost, our souls inspire		
	509	Spirit divine, attend our prayers		
	513	Like the murmur of the dove's song		
	704	O thou who camest from above		
3:13–17	116	"I come," the great Redeemer cries	Proper 18—Saturday	3 Easter—Wednesday
	120	The sinless one to Jordan came		
	121	Christ, when for us you were baptized		
	131, 132	When Christ's appearing was made known (st. 3)		
	135	Songs of thankfulness and praise (st. 2)		
	139	When Jesus went to Jordan's stream		
	448, 449	O love, how deep, how broad, how high		

Lectionary A	Lectionary B	Lectionary C	Pastoral Offices & Episcopal Services	Book of Occasional Services	Lesser Feasts and Fasts
See Above	See Above	See Above			
2 Advent					
,,　　　,,					
,,　　　,,					
,,　　　,,					
,,　　　,,					
1 Epiphany				Baptism of Our Lord	

			Daily Office Year One	Daily Office Year Two
3:16	509	Spirit divine, attend our prayers	See Above	See Above
	510	Come, Holy Spirit, heavenly Dove		
	512	Come, gracious Spirit, heavenly Dove		
	513	Like the murmur of the dove's song		
4:1–17	120	The sinless one to Jordan came (st. 4)	Proper 19—Monday Proper 19—Tuesday	3 Easter—Thursday 3 Easter—Friday
4:1–11	142	Lord, who throughout these forty days	Proper 19—Monday	3 Easter—Thursday
	143	The glory of these forty days		
	146, 147	Now let us all with one accord		
	150	Forty days and forty nights		
	284	O ye immortal throng (st. 3)		
	443	From God Christ's deity came forth		
	448, 449	O love, how deep, how broad, how high		
4:4	343	Shepherd of souls, refresh and bless	,, ,,	,, ,,
	627	Lamp of our feet, whereby we trace		
4:16	125, 126	The people who in darkness walked	Proper 19—Tuesday	3 Easter—Friday
	381	Thy strong word did cleave the darkness		
4:18–22	276	For thy blest saints, a noble throng (st. 2)	Proper 19—Wednesday	3 Easter—Saturday
	652, 653	Dear Lord and Father of mankind (st. 2)		
	661	They cast their nets in Galilee		
4:18–20	231, 232	By all your saints still striving (Saint Andrew)	,, ,,	,, ,,
	549, 550	Jesus calls us; o'er the tumult		
4:23–25	139	When Jesus went to Jordan's stream (st. 2)	,, ,,	,, ,,
	567	Thine arm, O Lord, in days of old		

Lectionary A	Lectionary B	Lectionary C	Pastoral Offices & Episcopal Services	Book of Occasional Services	Lesser Feasts and Fasts
See Above				See Above	
1 Lent					
,, ,,					
,, ,,					
3 Epiphany					
3 Epiphany St. Andrew	St. Andrew	St. Andrew			
,, ,,	,, ,,	,, ,,			
,, ,,					

			Daily Office Year One	**Daily Office Year Two**
5:3–12	**560**	Remember your servants, Lord	7 Epiphany—Monday Proper 19—Thursday	4 Easter—Monday
5:8	**656**	Blest are the pure in heart	,, ,,	,, ,,
6:10	**340, 341** **615** **573** **613**	For the bread which you have broken "Thy kingdom come!" on bended knee Father eternal, Ruler of creation (Refrain) Thy kingdom come, O God	8 Epiphany—Monday Proper 20—Friday	5 Easter—Tuesday
6:11	**709**	O God of Bethel, by whose hand	,, ,,	,, ,,
6:12–15	**581** **674**	Where charity and love prevail "Forgive our sins as we forgive"	,, ,,	,, ,,
6:25–33	**667** **709**	Sometimes a light surprises (st. 3) O God of Bethel, by whose hand	8 Epiphany—Wednesday Proper 21—Monday	5 Easter—Thursday
6:33	**711**	Seek ye first the kingdom of God	,, ,,	,, ,,
7:7	**711**	Seek ye first the kingdom of God	8 Epiphany—Thursday 5 Easter—Sunday Proper 21—Tuesday	5 Easter—Friday
7:15–20	**344** **392**	Lord, dismiss us with thy blessing Come, we that love the Lord	8 Epiphany—Friday 4 Easter—Sunday Proper 21—Wednesday	5 Easter—Saturday

Lectionary A	Lectionary B	Lectionary C	Pastoral Offices & Episcopal Services	Book of Occasional Services	Lesser Feasts and Fasts
4 Epiphany All Saints' Day At Confirmation	All Saints' Day At Confirmation	All Saints' Day At Confirmation	Marriage	All Saints' Day	George Herbert John Keble
,, ,,	,, ,,	,, ,,	,, ,,	,, ,,	,, ,,
					1 Lent—Tuesday
					,, ,,
					,, ,,
8 Epiphany Proper 3 Thanksgiving Day Of a Monastic II	Thanksgiving Day Of a Monastic II	Thanksgiving Day Of a Monastic II		Rogation Procession Celebration for a Home	Cuthbert
,, ,,	,, ,,	,, ,,		,, ,,	,, ,,
					1 Lent—Thursday
		Consecration of a Church			

			Daily Office Year One	Daily Office Year Two
7:24–27	636, 637	How firm a foundation, ye saints of the Lord	8 Epiphany—Saturday 4 Easter—Sunday Proper 21—Thursday	6 Easter—Friday
7:24–25	522, 523	Glorious things of thee are spoken	,, ,,	,, ,,
8:1–17	567	Thine arm, O Lord, in days of old	Proper 21—Friday	6 Easter—Saturday 7 Easter—Monday
8:5–13	135	Songs of thankfulness and praise (st. 3)	,, ,,	,, ,,
8:20	458	My song is love unknown	Proper 21—Saturday	7 Easter—Tuesday
8:23–27	608	Eternal Father, strong to save	,, ,,	,, ,,
8:28—9:8	567	Thine arm, O Lord, in days of old	Proper 22—Monday Proper 22—Tuesday	7 Easter—Wednesday 7 Easter—Thursday
9:1–8	135	Songs of thankfulness and praise (st. 3)	Proper 22—Tuesday	7 Easter—Thursday
9:9–13	706	In your mercy, Lord, you called me	Proper 22—Wednesday	7 Easter—Friday
9:9	231, 232 281	By all your saints still striving (Saint Matthew) He sat to watch o'er customs paid	,, ,,	,, ,,
9:18–35	567	Thine arm, O Lord, in days of old	Proper 22—Thursday Proper 22—Friday Eves of Apostles and Evangelists	Proper 1—Monday Eves of Apostles and Evangelists

Lectionary A	Lectionary B	Lectionary C	Pastoral Offices & Episcopal Services	Book of Occasional Services	Lesser Feasts and Fasts
Proper 4			Marriage		
,, ,,			,, ,,		
			Ministration to the Sick	Public Service of Healing	
Proper 5 St. Matthew	St. Matthew	St. Matthew			Friday after Ash Wednesday
,, ,,	,, ,,	,, ,,			
Proper 6					

			Daily Office Year One	Daily Office Year Two
9:18–26	493	O for a thousand tongues to sing	Proper 22—Thursday	
9:20–22	590	O Jesus Christ, may grateful hymns be rising	" "	
9:27–30	493 633	O for a thousand tongues to sing Word of God, come down to earth	Proper 22—Friday	Proper 1—Monday
9:36	472	Hope of the world, thou Christ of great compassion	Proper 22—Saturday Eves of Apostles and Evangelists	Proper 1—Tuesday Eves of Apostles and Evangelists
9:37–38	540 541	Awake, thou Spirit of the watchmen Come, labor on	" "	" "
10:7–8	528	Lord, you give the great commission	Proper 23—Monday	Proper 1—Wednesday
10:10	424	For the fruit of all creation	" "	" "
10:22	655	O Jesus, I have promised	Proper 23—Tuesday St. James—Evening Prayer St. James of Jerusalem—Morning Prayer	Proper 1—Thursday St. James—Evening Prayer St. James of Jerusalem—Morning Prayer
10:34–36	661	They cast their nets in Galilee	Proper 23—Thursday	Proper 1—Saturday
10:38–39	572	Weary of all trumpeting (st. 3)	" "	" "

Lectionary A	Lectionary B	Lectionary C	Pastoral Offices & Episcopal Services	Book of Occasional Services	Lesser Feasts and Fasts
Proper 6 For the Ministry II	For the Ministry II	For the Ministry II	Ordination: Priest		Charles Henry Brent Consecration of Samuel Seabury
,, ,,	,, ,,	,, ,,	,, ,,		,, ,,
,, ,, St. Barnabas	St. Barnabas	St. Barnabas			George Augustus Selwyn
,, ,,	,, ,,	,, ,,			,, ,,
Proper 7 Conversion of St. Paul Of a Martyr I	Conversion of St. Paul Of a Martyr I	Conversion of St. Paul Of a Martyr I			Fabian Athanasius James Hannington Edmund (General Convention 85)
Proper 8 For Social Justice	For Social Justice	For Social Justice			William Laud Alban
,, ,,	,, ,,	,, ,,			,, ,,

			Daily Office Year One	Daily Office Year Two
10:38	**484, 485** 675	Praise the Lord through every nation Take up your cross, the Savior said	See Above	See Above
10:42	**609**	Where cross the crowded ways of life	7 Easter—Sunday Proper 23—Thursday	,, ,,
11:2–6	**139** 458	When Jesus went to Jordan's stream (st. 2) My song is love unknown	3 Advent—Friday Proper 23—Friday Nativity of St. John the Baptist— Evening Prayer	Proper 2—Monday Nativity of St. John the Baptist— Evening Prayer
11:2–5	**493**	O for a thousand tongues to sing	,, ,,	,, ,,
11:7–15	**271, 272**	The great forerunner of the morn (st. 4)	3 Advent—Friday Proper 23—Saturday Nativity of St. John the Baptist— Evening Prayer	Proper 2—Tuesday Nativity of St. John the Baptist— Evening Prayer
11:7–10	**65** 67 70 75 76	Prepare the way, O Zion Comfort, comfort ye my people Herald, sound the note of judgment There's a voice in the wilderness crying On Jordan's bank the Baptist's cry	,, ,,	,, ,,
11:15	**536**	God has spoken to his people	,, ,,	,, ,,
11:28–30	**74**	Blest be the King whose coming (st. 4)	Proper 24—Tuesday	Proper 2—Thursday
11:28	**342** 644 692	O Bread of life, for sinners broken How sweet the Name of Jesus sounds I heard the voice of Jesus say (st. 1)	,, ,,	,, ,,

Lectionary A	Lectionary B	Lectionary C	Pastoral Offices & Episcopal Services	Book of Occasional Services	Lesser Feasts and Fasts
See Above	See Above	See Above			See Above
,, ,,	,, ,,	,, ,,			,, ,,
3 Advent					
,, ,,					
,, ,,					
,, ,,					
Proper 9 For Education	For Education	For Education		All Saints' Day	Anselm Francis of Assisi
,, ,,	,, ,,	,, ,,		,, ,,	,, ,,

			Daily Office Year One	Daily Office Year Two
12:9–22	**567**	Thine arm, O Lord, in days of old	The Epiphany Proper 24—Wednesday Proper 24—Thursday Proper 24—Friday	The Epiphany Proper 2—Friday Proper 2—Saturday Proper 2—Monday
12:22	**493** **633**	O for a thousand tongues to sing Word of God, come down on earth	Proper 24—Friday	Proper 2—Monday
12:33–35	**344** **392**	Lord, dismiss us with thy blessing Come, we that love the Lord	Proper 3—Sunday Proper 24—Saturday	Proper 3—Tuesday
13:3–43	**541** **588, 589**	Come, labor on Almighty God, your word is cast	6 Easter—Sunday Proper 25—Tuesday Proper 25—Wednesday Proper 25—Thursday Proper 25—Friday Proper 25—Saturday Proper 26—Monday	6 Easter—Monday 6 Easter—Tuesday Proper 3—Thursday Proper 3—Friday Proper 3—Saturday
13:9	**536**	God has spoken to his people	,, ,,	,, ,,
13:24–30, 36–43	**290**	Come, ye thankful people, come (sts. 2–4)	6 Easter—Sunday Proper 25—Friday Proper 26—Monday	Proper 3—Thursday
13:31–33	**24**	The day thou gavest, Lord, is ended	6 Easter—Sunday Proper 25—Saturday	Proper 3—Friday
13:43	**536**	God has spoken to his people	Proper 26—Monday	Proper 3—Saturday
13:55	**231, 232** **260**	By all your saints still striving (Saint Joseph) Come now, and praise the humble saint	Proper 4—Sunday Proper 26—Wednesday	Proper 4—Tuesday

Lectionary A	Lectionary B	Lectionary C	Pastoral Offices & Episcopal Services	Book of Occasional Services	Lesser Feasts and Fasts
Proper 10					
,, ,,					
Proper 11					
Proper 12					
Proper 11					
St. James of Jerusalem	St. James of Jerusalem	St. James of Jerusalem			

			Daily Office Year One	Daily Office Year Two
14:22–33	**608** **689**	Eternal Father, strong to save I sought the Lord, and afterward I knew	Proper 26—Saturday	Proper 4—Friday
14:34–36	**567** **590**	Thine arm, O Lord, in days of old O Jesus Christ, may grateful hymns be rising	" "	" "
15:30–31	**567**	Thine arm, O Lord, in days of old	Proper 5—Sunday Proper 27—Wednesday	Proper 5—Tuesday
15:32	**472**	Hope of the world, thou Christ of great compassion	" "	" "
16:13–20	**443**	From God Christ's deity came forth	Proper 27—Friday	Proper 5—Thursday
16:13–19	**254**	You are the Christ, O Lord	" "	" "
16:15–18	**525**	The Church's one foundation	" "	" "
16:18	**522, 523** **562**	Glorious things of thee are spoken Onward, Christian soldiers	" "	" "
16:24–26	**572**	Weary of all trumpeting (st. 3)	Proper 27—Saturday	Proper 5—Friday
16:24	**10** **484, 485** **675**	New every morning is the love Praise the Lord through every nation Take up your cross, the Savior said	" "	" "

Lectionary A	Lectionary B	Lectionary C	Pastoral Offices & Episcopal Services	Book of Occasional Services	Lesser Feasts and Fasts
Proper 14					
Proper 16 Confession of St. Peter	Confession of St. Peter	Confession of St. Peter			
,, ,,	,, ,,	,, ,,			
,, ,,	,, ,,	,, ,,			
,, ,,	,, ,,	,, ,,			
Proper 17 At Confirmation For the Ministry III	At Confirmation For the Ministry III	At Confirmation For the Ministry III		Special Vocation	
,, ,,	,, ,,	,, ,,		,, ,,	

			Daily Office Year One	Daily Office Year Two
17:1–8	**129, 130**	Christ upon the mountain peak	Proper 28—Monday	Proper 5—Saturday
	133, 134	O Light of Light, Love given birth		
	135	Songs of thankfulness and praise (st. 4)		
	136, 137	O wondrous type! O vision fair		
17:14–21	**567**	Thine arm, O Lord, in days of old	Proper 28—Tuesday	Proper 6—Monday
18:19–20	**518**	Christ is made the sure foundation	Proper 28—Friday	Proper 6—Thursday
18:21–35	**581**	Where charity and love prevail	Proper 28—Saturday	Proper 6—Friday
	674	"Forgive our sins as we forgive"		
19:1–6	**350**	O God of love, to thee we bow	Proper 29—Monday	Proper 6—Saturday
	352	O God, to those who here profess		
19:13–15	**480**	When Jesus left his Father's throne	Proper 29—Tuesday	Proper 7—Monday
19:16–30	**655**	O Jesus, I have promised	Proper 7—Sunday	,, ,,
			Proper 29—Tuesday	
			Proper 29—Wednesday	
20:17–19	**208**	The strife is o'er, the battle won	Proper 29—Friday	Proper 7—Thursday
20:20–23	**231, 232**	By all your saints still striving (Saint James)	,, ,,	,, ,,
	276	For thy blest saints, a noble throng		
20:29–34	**493**	O for a thousand tongues to sing	Proper 29—Saturday	Proper 7—Friday
	567	Thine arm, O Lord, in days of old		
	633	Word of God, come down on earth		

Lectionary A	Lectionary B	Lectionary C	Pastoral Offices & Episcopal Services	Book of Occasional Services	Lesser Feasts and Fasts
Last Epiphany					
Proper 18					
Proper 19					3 Lent—Tuesday
				Special Vocation	Aidan Hilda
St. James	St. James	St. James			2 Lent—Wednesday Polycarp

			Daily Office Year One	Daily Office Year Two
21:1–17	**486**	Hosanna to the living Lord	Palm Sunday	1 Advent—Monday 1 Advent—Tuesday Proper 7—Saturday Proper 8—Monday
21:1–11	**50**	This is the day the Lord hath made (sts. 3–5)		,, ,,
	65	Prepare the way, O Zion		
	71, 72	Hark! the glad sound! the Savior comes (st. 4)		
	74	Blest be the King whose coming		
	154, 155	All glory, laud, and honor		
	156	Ride on! ride on in majesty		
	458	My song is love unknown		
	480	When Jesus left his Father's throne		
21:1–9	**104**	A stable lamp is lighted (st. 2)		,, ,,
21:13	**51**	We the Lord's people, heart and voice uniting	,, ,,	1 Advent—Tuesday Proper 8—Monday
21:22	**518**	Christ is made the sure foundation		,, ,,
22:1–14	**339**	Deck thyself, my soul, with gladness	Proper 9—Sunday	1 Advent—Friday Proper 8—Thursday
22:32	**401**	The God of Abraham praise		2 Advent—Monday Proper 8—Saturday
22:37–40	**551**	Rise up, ye saints of God		2 Advent—Tuesday
	581	Where charity and love prevail		Proper 8—Saturday

Lectionary A	Lectionary B	Lectionary C	Pastoral Offices & Episcopal Services	Book of Occasional Services	Lesser Feasts and Fasts
Palm Sunday			Consecration of a Church		William Augustus Muhlenberg
,, ,,					
,, ,,					
Anniversary of the Dedication of a Church	Anniversary of the Dedication of a Church	Anniversary of the Dedication of a Church	,, ,,		,, ,,
Proper 23					
Proper 25 Human Rights (GC 82)	Human Rights (GC 82)	Human Rights (GC 82)			

			Daily Office Year One	Daily Office Year Two
22:41–46	450, 451	All hail the power of Jesus' Name		2 Advent—Tuesday 6 Easter—Saturday
23:37–39	590	O Jesus Christ, may grateful hymns be rising	Proper 10—Sunday	2 Advent—Friday Proper 9—Wednesday
24:1–2	598	Lord Christ, when first thou cam'st to earth (st. 2)		2 Advent—Saturday Proper 9—Thursday
24:12–13	53	Once he came in blessing		,, ,,
24:30	57, 58 454	Lo! he comes, with clouds descending Jesus came, adored by angels		3 Advent—Monday Proper 9—Friday
25:1–13	61, 62 68	"Sleepers, wake!" A voice astounds us Rejoice! rejoice, believers	1 Advent—Sunday	3 Advent—Thursday Proper 10—Monday
25:31–46	421 481 609 610	All glory be to God on high Rejoice, the Lord is King Where cross the crowded ways of life Lord, whose love through humble service	Proper 12—Sunday	3 Advent—Saturday Proper 10—Wednesday

Lectionary A	Lectionary B	Lectionary C	Pastoral Offices & Episcopal Services	Book of Occasional Services	Lesser Feasts and Fasts
St. Stephen *	St. Stephen	St. Stephen			
					Perpetua and her Companions The Martyrs of Uganda
Proper 27 Of a Saint III	Of a Saint III	Of a Saint III			
Proper 29 Of a Saint I World Hunger (GC 82)	Of a Saint I World Hunger (GC 82)	Of a Saint I World Hunger (GC 82)			1 Lent—Monday Richard William Wilberforce Martin of Tours Elizabeth Kamehamaha and Emma (GC 85)

			Daily Office Year One	Daily Office Year Two
26:26–29	51	We the Lord's people, heart and voice uniting		Proper 10—Saturday
	174	At the Lamb's high feast we sing		
	305, 306	Come, risen Lord, and deign to be our guest		
	320	Zion, praise thy Savior, singing		
	322	When Jesus died to save us		
	329, 330, 331	Now, my tongue, the mystery telling		
	340, 341	For the bread which you have broken		
	528	Lord, you give the great commission (st. 3)		
26:30	420	When in our music God is glorified (st. 4)		,, ,,
26:36–46	171	Go to dark Gethsemane (st. 1)		Proper 11—Monday
26:56	158	Ah, holy Jesus, how hast thou offended		Proper 11—Tuesday
	164	Alone thou goest forth, O Lord		
26:57—27:31	171	Go to dark Gethsemane (st. 2)		Proper 11—Wednesday
				Proper 11—Thursday
				Proper 11—Friday
				Proper 11—Saturday
				Proper 12—Monday
26:69–75	158	Ah, holy Jesus, how hast thou offended		,, ,,
	231, 232	By all your saints still striving (Confession of Saint Peter)		
27:15–26	158	Ah, holy Jesus, how has thou offended		,, ,,
	458	My song is love unknown		
27:27–54	168, 169	O sacred head, sore wounded		Proper 12—Tuesday
				Proper 12—Wednesday

Lectionary A	Lectionary B	Lectionary C	Pastoral Offices & Episcopal Services	Book of Occasional Services	Lesser Feasts and Fasts
				Public Service of Healing	
				,, ,,	
Palm Sunday				,, ,,	
,, ,,					
,, ,,					
,, ,,					
,, ,,					
,, ,,					

			Daily Office Year One	Daily Office Year Two
27:27–31	**170**	To mock your reign, O dearest Lord		See Above
	598	Lord Christ, when first thou cam'st to earth		
27:32–54	**171**	Go to dark Gethsemane (st. 3)		,, ,,
27:33–61	**172**	Were you there when they crucified my Lord		,, ,, Proper 12—Thursday
27:33–54	**165, 166**	Sing my tongue, the glorious battle		,, ,,
27:33–37	**167**	There is a green hill far away		,, ,,
27:45–50	**18**	As now the sun shines down at noon		,, ,,
27:45	**16, 17**	Now let us sing our praise to God		,, ,,
	23	The fleeting day is nearly gone		
	163	Sunset to sunrise changes now		
27:57–66	**458**	My song is love unknown		,, ,,
27:62–66	**173**	O sorrow deep		,, ,,

Lectionary A	Lectionary B	Lectionary C	Pastoral Offices & Episcopal Services	Book of Occasional Services	Lesser Feasts and Fasts
See Above					
,, ,,					
,, ,,					
,, ,,					
,, ,,					
,, ,,					
,, ,,					
,, ,, Holy Saturday	Holy Saturday	Holy Saturday			
,, ,,	,, ,,	,, ,,			

			Daily Office Year One	Daily Office Year Two
28:1–10	180	He is risen, he is risen		Easter Week—Wednesday
	183	Christians, to the Paschal victim		Proper 12—Friday
	184	Christ the Lord is risen again		
	190	Lift your voice rejoicing, Mary		
	193	That Easter day with joy was bright		
	196, 197	Look there! the Christ, our Brother, comes		
	199, 200	Come, ye faithful, raise the strain		
	201	On earth has dawned this day of days		
	203	O sons and daughters, let us sing (Easter Day)		
	205	Good Christians all, rejoice and sing		
	207	Jesus Christ is risen today		
	208	The strife is o'er, the battle done		
	210	The day of resurrection		
	231, 232	By all your saints still striving (Saint Mary Magdalene)		
28:1–8	673	The first one ever, oh ever, to know (st. 3)		,, ,,
28:1	47	On this day, the first of days		,, ,,
	48	O day of radiant gladness		
	50	This is the day the Lord hath made		
	51	We the Lord's people, heart and voice uniting		
	52	This day at thy creating word		
	452	Glorious the day when Christ was born		
28:2–7	284	O ye immortal throng (st. 6)		,, ,,
28:6	713	Christ is arisen		,, ,,
28:16–20	222	Rejoice, the Lord of life ascends	Ascension Day	Easter Week—Thursday
	460, 461	Alleluia! sing to Jesus (st. 2)		Ascension Day
				Proper 12—Saturday

Lectionary A	Lectionary B	Lectionary C	Pastoral Offices & Episcopal Services	Book of Occasional Services	Lesser Feasts and Fasts
Easter Day—Vigil, Early Service, and Principal Service Monday in Easter Week	Easter Day—Vigil, and Early Service Monday in Easter Week	Easter Day—Vigil, and Early Service Monday in Easter Week		Baptism of Our Lord All Saints' Day Vigil Before Baptism	
,, ,,	,, ,,	,, ,,		,, ,,	
,, ,,	,, ,,	,, ,,		,, ,,	
,, ,,	,, ,,	,, ,,		,, ,,	
,, ,,	,, ,,	,, ,,		,, ,,	
Trinity Sunday Of a Missionary II Of the Holy Trinity For the Mission of the Church II	Of a Missionary II Of the Holy Trinity For the Mission of the Church II	Of a Missionary II Of the Holy Trinity For the Mission of the Church II		,, ,,	Patrick Jackson Kemper Ninian

			Daily Office Year One	Daily Office Year Two
28:18	220, 221	O Lord Most High, eternal King	See Above	See Above
28:19–20	139	When Jesus went to Jordan's stream (st. 3)	,, ,,	,, ,,
	297	Descend O Spirit, purging flame		
	528	Lord, you give the great commission		
	531	O Spirit of the living God		
28:19	539	O Zion, haste, thy mission high fulfilling	,, ,,	,, ,,
28:20	182	Christ is alive! Let Christians sing	,, ,,	,, ,,
	342	O Bread of Life, for sinners broken		

Mark:

			Daily Office Year One	Daily Office Year Two
1:1–11	116	"I come," the great Redeemer cries	3 Advent—Wednesday	1 Lent—Monday
	120	The sinless one to Jordan came	1 Epiphany—Monday	
	121	Christ, when for us you were baptized	Proper 9—Friday	
	131, 132	When Christ's appearing was made known (st. 2)		
	135	Songs of thankfulness and praise (st. 2)		
	139	When Jesus went to Jordan's stream		
	448, 449	O love, how deep, how broad, how high		
1:1–8	69	What is the crying at the Jordan	,, ,,	,, ,,
	70	Herald, sound the note of judgment		
	76	On Jordan's bank the Baptist's cry		
1:1–5	59	Hark! a thrilling voice is sounding	,, ,,	,, ,,

Lectionary A	Lectionary B	Lectionary C	Pastoral Offices & Episcopal Services	Book of Occasional Services	Lesser Feasts and Fasts
See Above	See Above	See Above		See Above	See Above
,, ,,	,, ,,	,, ,,		,, ,,	,, ,,
,, ,,	,, ,,	,, ,,		,, ,,	,, ,,
				,, ,,	,, ,,
St. Mark At Baptism	2 Advent 1 Epiphany 1 Lent St. Mark At Baptism	St. Mark At Baptism		Baptism of Our Lord Vigil Before Baptism	
,, ,,	,, ,,	,, ,,		,, ,,	
,, ,,	,, ,,	,, ,,		Vigil Before Baptism	

			Daily Office Year One	Daily Office Year Two
1:1–4	67	Comfort, comfort ye my people	See Above	See Above
	75	There's a voice in the wilderness crying		
1:1–3	65	Prepare the way, O Zion	,, ,,	,, ,,
1:6	143	The glory of these forty days (st. 3)	,, ,,	,, ,,
1:10	509	Spirit divine, attend our prayer	,, ,,	,, ,,
	510	Come, Holy Spirit, heavenly Dove		
	512	Come, gracious Spirit, heavenly Dove		
	513	Like the murmur of the dove's song		
1:12–15	120	The sinless one to Jordan came (st. 4)	1 Epiphany—Monday Proper 9—Friday	1 Lent—Monday 1 Lent—Tuesday Proper 9—Sunday
1:12–13	142	Lord, who throughout these forty days	,, ,,	,, ,,
	143	The glory of these forty days		
	146, 147	Now let us all with one accord		
	150	Forty days and forty nights		
	284	O ye immortal throng (st. 3)		
	443	From God Christ's deity came forth		
	448, 449	O love, how deep, how broad, how high		
1:16–20	276	For thy blest saints, a noble throng (st. 2)	1 Epiphany—Tuesday Proper 9—Saturday St. James—Morning Prayer	1 Lent—Tuesday Proper 9—Sunday St. James—Morning Prayer
	652, 653	Dear Lord and Father of mankind (st. 2)		
	661	They cast their nets in Galilee		
1:16–18	231, 232	By all your saints still striving (Saint Andrew)	,, ,,	,, ,,
	549, 550	Jesus calls us; o'er the tumult		

Lectionary A		Lectionary B		Lectionary C		Pastoral Offices & Episcopal Services	Book of Occasional Services	Lesser Feasts and Fasts
See Above		See Above		See Above			See Above	
,,	,,	,,	,,	,,	,,		,,	,,
,,	,,	,,	,,	,,	,,		,,	,,
,,	,,	,,	,,	,,	,,		Baptism of Our Lord	
,,	,,	3 Epiphany 1 Lent		,,	,,			
,,	,,	,,	,,	,,	,,			
		,,	,,					
		,,	,,					

			Daily Office Year One	Daily Office Year Two
1:21—2:12	567	Thine arm, O Lord, in days of old	1 Epiphany—Tuesday 1 Epiphany—Wednesday Proper 9—Saturday Proper 10—Monday	1 Lent—Tuesday 1 Lent—Wednesday 1 Lent—Thursday Proper 10—Sunday Proper 11—Sunday
1:24	421	All glory be to God on high	,, ,,	,, ,,
2:1–12	135	Songs of thankfulness and praise (st. 3)	1 Epiphany—Thursday Proper 10—Tuesday	1 Lent—Thursday Proper 11—Sunday
2:13–14	231, 232 281	By all your saints still striving (Saint Matthew) He sat to watch o'er customs paid	1 Epiphany—Friday Proper 10—Wednesday	1 Lent—Friday
2:14–17	706	In your mercy, Lord, you called me	,, ,,	,, ,,
3:1–12	135 567	Songs of thankfulness and praise (st. 3) Thine arm, O Lord, in days of old	1 Epiphany—Saturday 2 Epiphany—Monday Proper 10—Thursday Proper 10—Friday	2 Epiphany—Sunday 1 Lent—Saturday 2 Lent—Monday
3:9–10	590	O Jesus Christ, may grateful hymns be rising	,, ,,	,, ,,
4:2–20	541 588, 589	Come, labor on Almighty God, your word is cast	2 Epiphany—Wednesday 2 Lent—Sunday Proper 11—Monday	2 Lent—Wednesday
4:9, 23	536	God has spoken to his people	,, ,,	,, ,,

Lectionary A	Lectionary B	Lectionary C	Pastoral Offices & Episcopal Services	Book of Occasional Services	Lesser Feasts and Fasts
For the Sick	4 Epiphany 5 Epiphany 6 Epiphany Proper 1 For the Sick	For the Sick		Public Service of Healing	
	,, ,,			,, ,,	
,, ,,	7 Epiphany Proper 2 For the Sick	,, ,,			
				Lay Ministries	
				,, ,,	

			Daily Office Year One	Daily Office Year Two
4:26–32	588, 589	Almighty God, your word is cast	2 Epiphany—Thursday Proper 11—Tuesday	2 Lent—Thursday
4:26–29	290	Come, ye thankful people, come (st. 2)	,, ,,	,, ,,
4:30–32	24	The day thou gavest, Lord, is ended	,, ,,	,, ,,
4:35–41	608	Eternal Father, strong to save	2 Epiphany—Friday Proper 11—Wednesday	2 Lent—Friday Proper 14—Sunday
5:1–43	567	Thine arm, O Lord, in days of old	2 Epiphany—Saturday 3 Epiphany—Monday 3 Lent—Sunday Proper 11—Thursday	2 Lent—Saturday
5:15	652, 653	Dear Lord and Father of mankind	2 Epiphany—Saturday 3 Lent—Sunday Proper 11—Thursday	2 Lent—Saturday
5:21–43	493	O for a thousand tongues to sing	3 Epiphany—Monday Proper 11—Friday	3 Lent—Monday Proper 15—Sunday
5:25–34	590	O Jesus Christ, may grateful hymns be rising	,, ,,	,, ,,
6:3	586 661	Jesus, thou divine Companion Christ the worker	3 Epiphany—Tuesday Proper 11—Saturday	3 Lent—Tuesday Proper 16—Sunday
6:34	472	Hope of the world, thou Christ of great compassion	3 Epiphany—Thursday Proper 12—Tuesday	3 Lent—Thursday 4 Easter—Sunday

Lectionary A	Lectionary B	Lectionary C	Pastoral Offices & Episcopal Services	Book of Occasional Services	Lesser Feasts and Fasts
For Rogation Days I	Proper 6 For Rogation Days I	For Rogation Days I			David James Lloyd Breck
,, ,,	,, ,,	,, ,,			,, ,,
,, ,,	,, ,,	,, ,,			,, ,,
	Proper 7				
	,, ,, Proper 8			Public Service of Healing	
	Proper 7			,, ,,	
	Proper 8			,, ,,	
	,, ,,				
	Proper 9				
	Proper 11				

			Daily Office Year One	Daily Office Year Two
6:47–52	608	Eternal Father, strong to save	3 Epiphany—Friday Proper 12—Wednesday	3 Lent—Friday
6:53–56	567	Thine arm, O Lord, in days of old	,, ,,	,, ,,
6:56	590	O Jesus Christ, may grateful hymns be rising	,, ,,	,, ,,
7:24–37	567	Thine arm, O Lord, in days of old	4 Epiphany—Monday Proper 12—Friday	3 Epiphany—Sunday 4 Lent—Monday
7:31–37	493 633	O for a thousand tongues to sing Word of God, come down on earth	,, ,,	,, ,,
8:22–26	493 567 633	O for a thousand tongues to sing Thine arm, O Lord, in days of old Word of God, come down on earth	4 Epiphany—Wednesday Proper 12—Tuesday	4 Epiphany—Sunday 4 Lent—Wednesday
8:27–30	254	You are the Christ, O Lord	4 Epiphany—Thursday Proper 13—Tuesday	4 Epiphany—Sunday 4 Lent—Thursday
8:34–36	572	Weary of all trumpeting (st. 3)	4 Epiphany—Thursday 5 Lent—Sunday Proper 13—Wednesday	4 Lent—Thursday
8:34	10 484, 485 675	New every morning is the love Praise the Lord through every nation Take up your cross, the Savior said	,, ,,	,, ,,

Lectionary A	Lectionary B	Lectionary C	Pastoral Offices & Episcopal Services	Book of Occasional Services	Lesser Feasts and Fasts
	Proper 12				
	Proper 18				
	,,　　　　,,				
Of a Martyr III	2 Lent Of a Martyr III	Of a Martyr III			The Martyrs of Japan The Martyrs of Lyons John Coleridge Patteson
,,　　　,,	,,　　　,,	,,　　　,,			,,　　　,,

			Daily Office Year One	Daily Office Year Two
9:2–8	129, 130 133, 134 135 136, 137	Christ upon the mountain peak O Light of Light, Love given birth Songs of thankfulness and praise (st. 4) O wondrous type! O vision fair	4 Epiphany—Friday Proper 13—Thursday	4 Lent—Friday
9:14–29	567	Thine arm, O Lord, in days of old	4 Epiphany—Saturday Proper 13—Friday	4 Lent—Saturday
9:35	659, 660	O Master, let me walk with thee	5 Epiphany—Monday Proper 13—Saturday	5 Lent—Monday
9:41	609	Where cross the crowded ways of life	” ”	” ”
10:2–9	350 352	O God of love, to thee we bow O God, to those who here profess	5 Epiphany—Wednesday Proper 14—Monday	5 Lent—Wednesday
10:13–16	480	When Jesus left his Father's throne	5 Epiphany—Wednesday Proper 14—Tuesday Holy Innocents—Evening Prayer	5 Epiphany—Sunday 5 Lent—Wednesday Holy Innocents—Evening Prayer
10:17–31	655	O Jesus, I have promised	5 Epiphany—Thursday Proper 14—Wednesday	5 Epiphany—Sunday
10:33–34	208	The strife is o'er, the battle done	5 Epiphany—Friday Proper 14—Thursday	6 Epiphany—Sunday 5 Lent—Thursday
10:35–40	231, 232 276	By all your saints still striving (Saint James) For thy blest saints, a noble throng	” ”	7 Epiphany—Sunday 5 Lent—Friday

Lectionary A	Lectionary B	Lectionary C	Pastoral Offices & Episcopal Services	Book of Occasional Services	Lesser Feasts and Fasts
	Last Epiphany				
	Proper 19				
	Proper 20				
	Proper 21				
	Proper 22		Marriage		
At Baptism	At Baptism	At Baptism	" "		Nicholas
	Proper 23				Antony
For All Baptized Christians	Proper 24 For All Baptized Christians	For All Baptized Christians			

			Daily Office Year One	Daily Office Year Two
10:43–45	**659, 660**	O Master, let me walk with thee	See Above	See Above
10:46–52	**493**	O for a thousand tongues to sing	5 Epiphany—Saturday	8 Epiphany—Sunday
	567	Thine arm, O Lord, in days of old	Proper 14—Friday	5 Lent—Saturday
	633	Word of God, come down on earth		
11:1–11	**486**	Hosanna to the living Lord	6 Epiphany—Monday	
			Proper 14—Saturday	
11:1–10	**50**	This is the day the Lord hath made (sts. 3–5)	,, ,,	
	65	Prepare the way, O Zion		
	71, 72	Hark! the glad sound! the Savior comes (st. 4)		
	74	Blest be the King whose coming		
	104	A stable lamp is lighted (st. 2)		
	154, 155	All glory, laud, and honor		
	156	Ride on! ride on in majesty		
	458	My song is love unknown		
	480	When Jesus left his Father's throne		
11:17	**51**	We the Lord's people, heart and voice uniting	6 Epiphany—Tuesday	Holy Week—Monday
			Proper 15—Monday	
11:24	**518**	Christ is made the sure foundation	,, ,,	,, ,,
	711	Seek ye first the Kingdom of God		
11:25–26	**674**	Forgive our sins as we forgive	,, ,,	,, ,,
11:25	**581**	Where charity and love prevail	,, ,,	,, ,,

Lectionary A	Lectionary B	Lectionary C	Pastoral Offices & Episcopal Services	Book of Occasional Services	Lesser Feasts and Fasts
See Above For Social Service	See Above For Social Service	See Above For Social Service			Gregory the Great
,, ,,	,, ,, Proper 25	,, ,,			
	Palm Sunday Proper 29				
	,, ,,				
Tuesday in Holy Week	Tuesday in Holy Week	Tuesday in Holy Week			

			Daily Office Year One	Daily Office Year Two
12:29–31	551	Rise up, ye saints of God	6 Epiphany—Friday	
	581	Where charity and love prevail	Proper 15—Thursday	
12:35–37	450, 451	All hail the power of Jesus' Name	6 Epiphany—Saturday Proper 15—Friday	
13:1–2	598	Lord Christ, when first thou cam'st to earth (st. 2)	Proper 15—Saturday	
13:13	655	O Jesus, I have promised	Proper 15—Saturday	
13:24–29	454	Jesus came, adored by angels	Proper 16—Monday Proper 16—Tuesday St. Michael & All Angels—Evening Prayer	St. Michael & All Angels—Evening Prayer
13:24–27	57, 58	Lo! he comes, with clouds descending	,, ,,	,, ,,
13:32–37	61, 62	"Sleepers, wake!" A voice astounds us	Proper 16—Tuesday	
	68	Rejoice! rejoice, believers		
14:15–25	305, 306	Come, risen Lord, and deign to be our guest	Proper 16—Thursday	Maundy Thursday
14:22–25	51	We the Lord's people, heart and voice uniting	,, ,,	,, ,,
	174	At the Lamb's high feast we sing		
	320	Zion, praise thy Savior, singing		
	322	When Jesus died to save us		
	329, 330, 321	Now, my tongue, the mystery telling		
	340, 341	For the bread which you have broken		

Lectionary A	Lectionary B	Lectionary C	Pastoral Offices & Episcopal Services	Book of Occasional Services	Lesser Feasts and Fasts
	Proper 26				3 Lent—Friday Aelred (GC 85)
	1 Advent				
	,, ,,				
	,, ,,				

			Daily Office Year One	Daily Office Year Two
14:24–25	528	Lord, you give the great commission (st. 3)	See Above	See Above
14:26	420	When in our music God is glorified (st. 4)	” ”	
14:32–42	171	Go to dark Gethsemane (st. 1)	Proper 16—Friday	
14:50	158 164	Ah, holy Jesus, how hast thou offended Alone thou goest forth, O Lord	Proper 16—Saturday	
14:53—15:20	171	Go to dark Gethsemane (st. 2)	Proper 17—Monday	
14:53–72	158	Ah, holy Jesus, how hast thou offended	” ”	
14:62	57, 58 454	Lo! he comes, with clouds descending Jesus came, adored by angels	” ”	
14:66–72	231, 232	By all your saints still striving (Confession of Saint Peter)	Proper 17—Tuesday	
15:6–15	158 458	Ah, holy Jesus, how hast thou offended My song is love unknown	Proper 17—Wednesday Proper 17—Thursday	
15:16–39	168, 169	O sacred head, sore wounded	Proper 17—Thursday Proper 17—Friday Proper 17—Saturday	
15:16–20	170 598	To mock your reign, O dearest Lord Lord Christ, when first thou cam'st to earth	Proper 17—Thursday	

Lectionary A	Lectionary B	Lectionary C	Pastoral Offices & Episcopal Services	Book of Occasional Services	Lesser Feasts and Fasts
	Palm Sunday				
	,, ,,				
	,, ,,				
	,, ,,				
	,, ,,				
	,, ,,				
	,, ,,				
	,, ,,				

			Daily Office Year One	Daily Office Year Two
15:21–39	**165, 166** **171**	Sing, my tongue, the glorious battle Go to dark Gethsemane (st. 3)	Proper 17—Friday Proper 17—Saturday	
15:22–47	**172**	Were you there when they crucified my Lord	Proper 17—Friday Proper 17—Saturday Proper 18—Monday	
15:22–28	**167**	There is a green hill far away	Proper 17—Friday	
15:25	**12, 13**	The golden sun lights up the sky	" "	
15:33–36	**18**	As now the sun shines down at noon	Proper 17—Saturday	
15:33	**16, 17** **23** **163**	Now let us sing our praise to God The fleeting day is nearly gone Sunset to sunrise changes now	" "	
15:42–47	**173** **458**	O sorrow deep My song is love unknown	Proper 18—Monday St. Mary Magdalene—Morning Prayer	St. Mary Magdalene—Morning Praye

Lectionary A	Lectionary B	Lectionary C	Pastoral Offices & Episcopal Services	Book of Occasional Services	Lesser Feasts and Fasts
	See Above				
	,, ,,				
	,, ,,				
	,, ,,				
	,, ,,				
	,, ,,				
	,, ,,				

			Daily Office Year One	Daily Office Year Two
16:1–11	**180**	He is risen, he is risen	Proper 18—Tuesday	Easter Week—Monday
	183	Christians, to the Paschal victim	St. Mary Magdalene—Morning Prayer	Easter Week—Tuesday
	184	Christ the Lord is risen again		3 Easter—Sunday
	190	Lift your voice rejoicing, Mary		St. Mary Magdalene—Morning Prayer
	196, 197	Look there! the Christ, our Brother, comes		
	199, 200	Come, ye faithful, raise the strain		
	201	On earth has dawned this day of days		
	203	O sons and daughters, let us sing (Easter Day)		
	205	Good Christians all, rejoice and sing		
	207	Jesus Christ is risen today		
	208	The strife is o'er, the battle done		
	210	The day of resurrection		
	231, 232	By all your saints still striving (Saint Mary Magdalene)		
	673	The first one ever, oh ever, to know (st. 3)		
16:2–9	**47**	On this day, the first of days	,, ,,	,, ,,
	48	O day of radiant gladness		
	50	This is the day the Lord hath made		
	51	We the Lord's people, heart and voice uniting		
	52	This day at thy creating word		
	452	Glorious the day when Christ was born		
16:5–7	**284**	O ye immortal throng (st. 6)	,, ,,	,, ,,
16:6	**713**	Christ is arisen	,, ,,	,, ,,
16:15–16	**139**	When Jesus went to Jordan's stream (st. 3)	,, ,,	,, ,,
	297	Descend, O Spirit, purging flame		
16:16	**298**	All who believe and are baptized	,, ,,	,, ,,

Lectionary A	Lectionary B	Lectionary C	Pastoral Offices & Episcopal Services	Book of Occasional Services	Lesser Feasts and Fasts
Saturday in Easter Week Ascension Day	Easter Day—Principal Service Saturday in Easter Week Ascension Day	Saturday in Easter Week Ascension Day			
,, ,,	,, ,,	,, ,,			
,, ,,	,, ,,	,, ,,			
,, ,,	,, ,,	,, ,,			
Saturday in Easter Week Ascension Day St. Mark	Saturday in Easter Week Ascension Day St. Mark	Saturday in Easter Week Ascension Day St. Mark			Cyril and Methodius
St. Mark	St. Mark	St. Mark			,, ,,

16:19	194, 195	Jesus lives! thy terrors now	See Above	See Above
	214	Hail the day that sees him rise		
	215	See the Conqueror mounts in triumph		
	217, 218	A hymn of glory let us sing		
	219	The Lord ascendeth up on high		
	220, 221	O Lord Most High, eternal King		
	222	Rejoice, the Lord of life ascends		
	460, 461	Alleluia! sing to Jesus		

Luke:

1:1–4	285	What thanks and praise to thee we owe	St. Luke—Morning Prayer	4 Advent—Monday Proper 20—Monday St. Luke—Morning Prayer
1:5–25, 57–80	231, 232	By all your saints still striving (The Nativity of Saint John the Baptist)	4 Advent—Tuesday 4 Advent—Friday	2 Advent—Sunday 4 Advent—Monday
	271, 272	The great forerunner of the morn	Eve of St. John the Baptist	4 Advent—Thursday 4 Advent—Friday Eve of St. John the Baptist
1:5–38	282, 283	Christ, the fair glory of the holy angels (st. 3)	,,　　　,,	4 Advent—Monday 4 Advent—Tuesday
1:26–56	265	The angel Gabriel from heaven came	4 Advent—Wednesday	4 Advent—Tuesday
	268, 269	Ye who claim the faith of Jesus		4 Advent—Wednesday
	618	Ye watchers and ye holy ones		

Lectionary A	Lectionary B	Lectionary C	Pastoral Offices & Episcopal Services	Book of Occasional Services	Lesser Feasts and Fasts
Ascension Day St. Mark	Ascension Day St. Mark	Ascension Day St. Mark			See Above
Nativity of St. John the Baptist	Nativity of St. John the Baptist	Nativity of St. John the Baptist		Advent Festival Christmas Festival	
The Annunciation	4 Advent The Annunciation	The Annunciation		,, ,,	Parents of the Blessed Virgin Mary
,, ,, The Visitation St. Mary the Virgin Of the Incarnation Oppression (GC 82)	,, ,, The Visitation St. Mary the Virgin Of the Incarnation Oppression (GC 82)	,, ,, 4 Advent The Visitation St. Mary the Virgin Of the Incarnation Oppression (GC 82)		,, ,,	,, ,,

			Daily Office Year One	Daily Office Year Two
1:26–38	54	Savior of the nations, come	See Above	See Above
	55	Redeemer of the nations, come		
	60	Creator of the stars of night		
	77	From east to west, from shore to shore (sts. 1–3)		
	81	Lo, how a Rose e'er blooming		
	82	Of the Father's love begotten (st. 2)		
	248, 249	To the Name of our salvation		
	252	Jesus! Name of wondrous love		
	258	Virgin-born, we bow before thee		
	263, 264	The Word whom earth and sea and sky		
	266	Nova, nova		
	267	Praise we the Lord this day		
	270	Gabriel's message does away		
	278	Sing we of the blessed Mother		
	231, 232	By all your saints still striving (Saint Mary the Virgin)		
	673	The first one ever, oh, ever to know (st. 1)		
1:31	435	At the Name of Jesus	„ „	„ „
	475	God himself is with us		
1:46–55	437, 438	Tell out, my soul, the greatness of the Lord	4 Advent—Thursday Proper 13—Sunday	4 Advent—Wednesday
1:68–79	444	Blessed be the God of Israel	December 24	4 Advent—Friday
1:78–79	6, 7	Christ, whose glory fills the skies	„ „	„ „
	56	O come, O come, Emmanuel		
1:79	703	Lead us, O Father, in the paths of peace	„ „	„ „

Lectionary A	Lectionary B	Lectionary C	Pastoral Offices & Episcopal Services	Book of Occasional Services	Lesser Feasts and Fasts
See Above	See Above	See Above		See Above	See Above
,, ,,	,, ,,	,, ,,		,, ,,	,, ,,
,, ,,	,, ,,	,, ,,		,, ,,	
Nativity of St. John the Baptist	Nativity of St. John the Baptist	Nativity of St. John the Baptist		Christmas Festival	
,, ,,	,, ,,	,, ,,		,, ,,	
,, ,,	,, ,,	,, ,,		,, ,,	

2:1–20	**77**	From east to west, from shore to shore
	78, 79	O little town of Bethlehem
	82	Of the Father's love begotten
	83	O come, all ye faithful
	91	Break forth, O beauteous heavenly light
	92	On this day earth shall ring
	93	Angels from the realms of glory
	96	Angels we have heard on high
	97	Dost thou in a manger lie
	98	Unto us a boy is born
	99	Go tell it on the mountain
	101	Away in a manger, no crib for his bed
	102	Once in royal David's city
	103	A child is born in Bethlehem
	104	A stable lamp is lighted
	106	Christians, awake, salute the happy morn
	107	Good Christian friends, rejoice
	110	The snow lay on the ground
	111	Silent night, holy night
	112	In the bleak midwinter
	114	'Twas in the moon of wintertime
	115	What child is this, who, laid to rest
	491	Where is this stupendous stranger
2:1–7	**452**	Glorious the day when Christ was born
2:4	**307**	Lord, enthroned in heavenly splendor
2:8–14	**80**	From heaven above to earth I come
	87	Hark! the herald angels sing
	89, 90	It came upon the midnight clear
	94, 95	While shepherds watched their flocks by night
	105	God rest you merry, gentlemen
	109	The first Nowell the angel did say

Lectionary A	Lectionary B	Lectionary C	Pastoral Offices & Episcopal Services	Book of Occasional Services	Lesser Feasts and Fasts
Christmas Day I & II Holy Name	Christmas Day I & II Holy Name	Christmas Day I & II Holy Name		See Above	
,, ,,	,, ,,	,, ,,		,, ,,	
,, ,,	,, ,,	,, ,,		,, ,,	

			Daily Office Year One	Daily Office Year Two
2:13–14	284	O ye immortal throng (st. 2)		
	307	Lord, enthroned in heavenly splendor		
	336	Come with us, O blessed Jesus		
2:14	421	All glory be to God on high		
	426	Songs of praise the angels sang (st. 2)		
2:21	248, 249	To the Name of our salvation		
	250	Now greet the swiftly changing year (st. 2)		
	252	Jesus! Name of wondrous love		
	435	At the Name of Jesus		
2:22–40	257	O Zion, open wide thy gates		First Sunday after Christmas
	259	Hail to the Lord who comes		
2:22–38	93	Angels, from the realms of glory (st. 4)		
2:29–32	499	Lord God, you now have set your servant free		
2:33–35	159	At the cross her vigil keeping		
	278	Sing we of the blessed Mother		
2:41–52	231, 232	By all your saints still striving (Saint Joseph)		
	260	Come now, and praise the humble saint		
	261, 262	By the Creator, Joseph was appointed		
2:52	480	When Jesus left his Father's throne		
	587	Our Father, by whose Name		
	611	Christ the worker		

Lectionary A	Lectionary B	Lectionary C	Pastoral Offices & Episcopal Services	Book of Occasional Services	Lesser Feasts and Fasts
See Above	See Above	See Above		See Above	
,, ,,	,, ,,	,, ,,		,, ,,	
Holy Name	Holy Name	Holy Name		,, ,,	
The Presentation	The Presentation	The Presentation		,, ,,	
,, ,,	,, ,,	,, ,,		,, ,,	
,, ,,	,, ,,	,, ,,		,, ,,	
,, ,,	,, ,,	,, ,,		,, ,,	
2 Christmas St. Joseph	2 Christmas St. Joseph	2 Christmas St. Joseph	Thanksgiving for a Child		
,, ,,	,, ,,	,, ,,			

			Daily Office Year One	Daily Office Year Two
3:1–20	59	Hark! a thrilling voice is sounding	3 Advent—Saturday	Proper 20—Monday
	69	What is the crying at Jordan	2 Easter—Thursday	Proper 20—Tuesday
	70	Herald, sound the note of judgment	Proper 20—Sunday	
	76	On Jordan's bank the Baptist's cry		
3:1–9	67	Comfort, comfort ye my people	,, ,,	,, ,,
	75	There's a voice in the wilderness crying		
3:4–5	65	Prepare the way, O Zion	,, ,,	,, ,,
3:16	500	Creator Spirit, by whose aid	2 Easter—Friday	,, ,,
	501, 502	O Holy Spirit, by whose breath	Proper 20—Sunday	
	503, 504	Come, Holy Ghost, our souls inspire		
	509	Spirit divine, attend our prayers		
	513	Like the murmur of the dove's song		
	704	O thou who camest from above		
3:21–22	116	"I come," the great Redeemer cries	2 Easter—Friday	,, ,,
	120	The sinless one to Jordan came	Proper 14—Sunday	
	121	Christ, when for us you were baptized		
	131, 132	When Christ's appearing was made known (st. 3)		
	135	Songs of thankfulness and praise (st. 2)		
	139	When Jesus went to Jordan's stream		
	448, 449	O love, how deep, how broad, how high		
	509	Spirit divine, attend our prayers		
	510	Come, Holy Spirit, heavenly Dove		
	512	Come, gracious Spirit, heavenly Dove		
	513	Like the murmur of the dove's song		
4:1–15	120	The sinless one to Jordan came (st. 4)	2 Easter—Saturday	Proper 20—Wednesday
				Proper 20—Thursday

Lectionary A	Lectionary B	Lectionary C	Pastoral Offices & Episcopal Services	Book of Occasional Services	Lesser Feasts and Fasts
		2 Advent 3 Advent		Baptism of Our Lord	
		" "			
		" "			
		3 Advent 1 Epiphany		" "	
		1 Epiphany		" "	
St. Luke	St. Luke	3 Epiphany 1 Lent St. Luke			

			Daily Office Year One	Daily Office Year Two
4:1–13	142 143 146, 147 150 443 448, 449	Lord, who throughout these forty days The glory of these forty days Now let us all with one accord Forty days and forty nights From God Christ's deity came forth O love, how deep, how broad, how high	See Above	See Above
4:4	343	Shepherd of souls, refresh and bless	,, ,,	,, ,,
4:16–21	71, 72	Hark! the glad sound! the Savior comes	3 Easter—Monday	5 Easter—Sunday Proper 20—Thursday
4:18–19	539	O Zion, haste, they mission high fulfilling	,, ,,	,, ,,
4:31–41	567	Thine arm, O Lord, in days of old	3 Easter—Tuesday 3 Easter—Wednesday	Proper 20—Friday
4:34	421	All glory be to God on high	3 Easter—Tuesday	,, ,,
5:1–11	276 661	For thy blest saints, a noble throng (st. 2) They cast their nets in Galilee	3 Easter—Thursday Proper 21—Sunday	Proper 21—Monday
5:11	652, 653	Dear Lord and Father of mankind (st. 2)	,, ,,	,, ,,
5:12–26	567	Thine arm, O Lord, in days of old	3 Easter—Friday	Proper 21—Tuesday
5:17–26	135	Songs of thankfulness and praise (st. 3)	,, ,,	,, ,,
5:27–32	706	In your mercy, Lord, you called me	3 Easter—Saturday	Proper 21—Wednesday

Lectionary A	Lectionary B	Lectionary C	Pastoral Offices & Episcopal Services	Book of Occasional Services	Lesser Feasts and Fasts
		1 Lent			
		" "			
St. Luke At Confirmation	St. Luke At Confirmation	3 Epiphany St. Luke At Confirmation		Consecration of Chrism	
" "	" "	" "		" "	
		5 Epiphany			Augustine of Canterbury
		" "			" "
					Saturday after Ash Wednesday

			Daily Office Year One	Daily Office Year Two
5:27–28	**231, 232**	By all your saints still striving (Saint Matthew)	See Above	See Above
	281	He sat to watch o'er customs paid		
6:6–11	**567**	Thine arm, O Lord, in days of old	4 Easter—Monday	Proper 21—Thursday
6:43–45	**344**	Lord, dismiss us with thy blessing	4 Easter—Thursday	Proper 22—Monday
	392	Come, we that love the Lord		
6:47–49	**636, 637**	How firm a foundation, ye saints of the Lord	,, ,,	,, ,,
7:1–23	**567**	Thine arm, O Lord, in days of old	4 Easter—Friday Proper 22—Sunday	Proper 22—Tuesday
7:1–17	**493**	O for a thousand tongues to sing	,, ,,	,, ,,
7:13–35	**271, 272**	The great forerunner of the morn (st. 4)	4 Easter—Saturday	Proper 22—Wednesday
7:18–23	**139**	When Jesus went to Jordan's stream (st. 2)	,, ,,	,, ,,
	458	My song is love unknown		
7:36–50	**643**	My God, how wonderful thou art	5 Easter—Monday Proper 23—Sunday	Proper 22—Thursday
8:1–3	**231, 232**	By all your saints still striving (Saint Mary Magdalene)	5 Easter—Tuesday	Proper 22—Friday
8:2	**567**	Thine arm, O Lord, in days of old	,, ,,	,, ,,

Lectionary A	Lectionary B	Lectionary C	Pastoral Offices & Episcopal Services	Book of Occasional Services	Lesser Feasts and Fasts
					See Above
		8 Epiphany Proper 3			Alfred the Great Clement of Rome
		,, ,,			,, ,,
		Proper 4 Proper 5			Monnica
					,, ,,
		Proper 6			

			Daily Office Year One	Daily Office Year Two
8:4–15	**541**	Come, labor on	5 Easter—Tuesday	See Above
	588, 589	Almighty God, your word is cast	Proper 16—Sunday	
8:8	**536**	God has spoken to his people	,, ,,	,, ,,
8:22–25	**608**	Eternal Father, strong to save	5 Easter—Wednesday	Proper 22—Saturday
8:26–56	**567**	Thine arm, O Lord, in days of old	5 Easter—Thursday	Proper 23—Monday
			5 Easter—Friday	Proper 23—Tuesday
			Proper 17—Sunday	
8:40–56	**493**	O for a thousand tongues to sing	5 Easter—Friday	,, ,,
			Proper 17—Sunday	
9:2	**528**	Lord, you give the great commission	5 Easter—Saturday	Proper 23—Wednesday
9:18–22	**254**	You are the Christ, O Lord	6 Easter—Monday	Last Epiphany—Sunday
				Proper 23—Thursday
9:23–25	**572**	Weary of all trumpeting (st. 3)	,, ,,	,, ,,
9:23	**10**	New every morning is the love	,, ,,	,, ,,
	484, 485	Praise the Lord through every nation		
	675	Take up your cross, the Savior said		
9:28–36	**129, 130**	Christ upon the mountain peak	6 Easter—Friday	Proper 23—Friday
	133, 134	O Light of Light, Love given birth		
	135	Songs of thankfulness and praise (st. 4)		
	136, 137	O wondrous type! O vision fair		

Lectionary A	Lectionary B	Lectionary C	Pastoral Offices & Episcopal Services	Book of Occasional Services	Lesser Feasts and Fasts
		Proper 7			Thursday after Ash Wednesday John and Charles Wesley
		,, ,,			,, ,,
		,, ,,			,, ,,
The Transfiguration	The Transfiguration	Last Epiphany The Transfiguration			

			Daily Office Year One	Daily Office Year Two
9:37–43	**567**	Thine arm, O Lord, in days of old	6 Easter—Saturday	Proper 23—Saturday
9:51	**559**	Lead us, heavenly Father, lead us	7 Easter—Monday	Proper 24—Monday
9:58	**458**	My song is love unknown	,, ,,	,, ,,
9:62	**564, 565** **655**	He who would valiant be O Jesus, I have promised	,, ,,	,, ,,
10:2	**540** **541**	Awake, thou Spirit of the watchmen Come, labor on	7 Easter—Tuesday Proper 24—Sunday	Proper 24—Tuesday
10:7	**424**	For the fruit of all creation	,, ,,	,, ,,
10:9	**528**	Lord, you give the great commission	,, ,,	,, ,,
10:25–37	**602**	Jesu, Jesu, fill us with your love	7 Easter—Thursday Proper 25—Sunday	Proper 3—Sunday Proper 24—Thursday
10:27	**551** **581**	Rise up, ye saints of God Where charity and love prevail	,, ,,	,, ,,
11:1	**698**	Eternal Spirit of the living Christ	6 Easter—Tuesday	Proper 4—Sunday Proper 24—Saturday

Lectionary A	Lectionary B	Lectionary C	Pastoral Offices & Episcopal Services	Book of Occasional Services	Lesser Feasts and Fasts
		Proper 8			
Of a Monastic I	Of a Monastic I	" " Of a Monastic I			
" "	" "	" "			
Of a Missionary I For the Mission of the Church I	Of a Missionary I For the Mission of the Church I	Proper 9 Of a Missionary I For the Mission of the Church I	New Ministry		Channing Moore Williams Thomas Bray David Pendleton Oakerhater (GC 85)
" "	" "	" "			" "
" "	" "	" "			" "
		Proper 10			Joseph Butler
		" "			" "
		Proper 12			Lancelot Andrewes

			Daily Office Year One	Daily Office Year Two
11:2	340, 341 573 613 615	For the bread which you have broken Father eternal, Ruler of creation (Refrain) Thy kingdom come, O God "Thy kingdom come!" on bended knee	See Above	See Above
11:3	709	O God of Bethel, by whose hand	,, ,,	,, ,,
11:4	581 674	Where charity and love prevail Forgive our sins as we forgive	,, ,,	,, ,,
11:9	711	Seek ye first the kingdom of God	,, ,,	,, ,,
11:14–15	567	Thine arm, O Lord, in days of old	7 Easter—Saturday	Proper 25—Monday
11:27–28	258	Virgin-born, we bow before thee	Proper 1—Monday	Proper 25—Tuesday
12:22–31	667 709	Sometimes a light surprises (st. 3) O God of Bethel, by whose hand	6 Easter—Wednesday Proper 1—Thursday Proper 26—Sunday	Proper 25—Friday
12:31	711	Seek ye first the kingdom of God	,, ,,	,, ,,
12:35–40	61, 62 68	"Sleepers, wake!" A voice astounds us Rejoice! rejoice, believers	Proper 1—Friday	Proper 5—Sunday Proper 25—Saturday
12:51–53	661	They cast their nets in Galilee	Proper 1—Friday	Proper 7—Sunday Proper 26—Monday
13:6–9	344 392	Lord, dismiss us with thy blessing Come, we that love the Lord	Proper 2—Monday	Proper 26—Tuesday

Lectionary A	Lectionary B	Lectionary C	Pastoral Offices & Episcopal Services	Book of Occasional Services	Lesser Feasts and Fasts
		See Above			See Above
		,, ,,			,, ,,
		,, ,,			,, ,,
Of the Holy Spirit	Of the Holy Spirit	,, ,, Of the Holy Spirit			
					3 Lent—Thursday
Of the Incarnation	Of the Incarnation	Of the Incarnation			
					1 Lent—Wednesday Cathering of Siena Louis
					,, ,,
Of a Monastic I	Of a Monastic I	Proper 14 Of a Monastic I	Ordination: Deacon	Lay Ministries	Ambrose Clare
		Proper 15			
		3 Lent			

			Daily Office Year One	Daily Office Year Two
13:10–17	**567**	Thine arm, O Lord, in days of old	Proper 2—Tuesday	Proper 8—Sunday Proper 26—Wednesday
13:18–21	**24**	The day thou gavest, Lord, is ended	Proper 2—Wednesday	Proper 26—Thursday
13:34–35	**590**	O Jesus Christ, may grateful hymns be rising	Proper 2—Thursday	Proper 26—Friday
14:1–6	**567**	Thine arm, O Lord, in days of old	Proper 2—Friday	Proper 26—Saturday
14:15–24	**339**	Deck thyself, my soul, with gladness	Proper 2—Saturday Proper 27—Sunday	Proper 27—Monday
14:27	**484, 485** **675**	Praise the Lord through every nation Take up your cross, the Savior said	Proper 3—Monday	Proper 27—Tuesday
15:3–7	**645, 646**	The King of love my shepherd is	Proper 3—Tuesday	Proper 27—Wednesday
16:19–31	**354** **356**	Into paradise may the angels lead you May choirs of angels lead you	Proper 3—Saturday	Proper 28—Monday
17:3–4	**674**	"Forgive our sins as we forgive"	Proper 4—Monday	Proper 28—Tuesday
17:11–19	**567**	Thine arm, O Lord, in days of old	Proper 4—Tuesday	Proper 28—Wednesday
18:15–17	**480**	When Jesus left his Father's throne	Proper 4—Saturday	Proper 29—Monday
18:18–30	**655**	O Jesus, I have promised	" "	" "
18:31–33	**208**	The strife is o'er, the battle done	Proper 5—Monday	Proper 29—Tuesday

Lectionary A	Lectionary B	Lectionary C	Pastoral Offices & Episcopal Services	Book of Occasional Services	Lesser Feasts and Fasts
		2 Lent			
		Proper 17			Chad
		Proper 18			Benedict of Nursia
		Proper 19		Special Vocation	
		Proper 21			2 Lent—Thursday
		Proper 22			
		Proper 23	Ministration to the Sick	Public Service of Healing	
		Thanksgiving for a Child			

			Daily Office Year One	**Daily Office Year Two**
18:35–43	493	O for a thousand tongues to sing	See Above	See Above
	567	Thine arm, O Lord, in days of old		
	633	Word of God, come down to earth		
19:29–46	486	Hosanna to the living Lord	Proper 5—Thursday	Palm Sunday
				Proper 29—Friday
				Proper 29—Saturday
19:29–40	104	A stable lamp is lighted (st. 2)	,, ,,	,, ,,
19:29–39	50	This is the day the Lord hath made (sts. 3–5)	,, ,,	,, ,,
	65	Prepare the way, O Zion		
	71, 72	Hark! the glad sound! the Savior comes (st. 4)		
	74	Blest be the King whose coming		
	154, 155	All glory, laud, and honor		
	156	Ride on! ride on in majesty		
	458	My song is love unknown		
	480	When Jesus left his Father's throne		
19:41–42	590	O Jesus Christ, may grateful hymns be rising	Proper 5—Friday	,, ,,
	609	Where cross the crowded ways of life		
19:43–44	598	Lord Christ, when first thou cam'st to earth (st. 2)	,, ,,	,, ,,
19:46	51	We the Lord's people, heart and voice uniting	,, ,,	,, ,,
20:41–44	450, 451	All hail the power of Jesus' Name	1 Advent—Friday	
			Proper 6—Thursday	

Lectionary A	Lectionary B	Lectionary C	Pastoral Offices & Episcopal Services	Book of Occasional Services	Lesser Feasts and Fasts
		Palm Sunday Proper 29			
		,, ,,			
		,, ,,			

			Daily Office Year One	Daily Office Year Two
21:6	**598**	Lord Christ, when first thou cam'st to earth (st. 2)	1 Advent—Saturday Proper 6—Friday	1 Advent—Sunday
21:19	**53**	Once he came in blessing	1 Advent—Saturday Proper 6—Friday The Patronal Feast—Evening Prayer	1 Advent—Sunday The Patronal Feast—Evening Prayer
21:25–28	**57, 58** **454**	Lo! he comes, with clouds descending Jesus came, adored by angels	2 Advent—Monday Proper 6—Saturday	
22:7–20	**305, 306**	Come, risen Lord, and deign to be our guest	2 Advent—Thursday Proper 7—Tuesday	
22:14–20	**51** **174** **320** **322** **329, 330, 331** **340, 341** **528**	We the Lord's people, heart and voice uniting At the Lamb's high feast we sing Zion, praise thy Savior, singing When Jesus died to save us Now my tongue, the mystery telling For the bread which you have broken Lord, you give the great commission (st. 3)	2 Advent—Friday Proper 7—Wednesday	
22:19	**342**	O Bread of life, for sinners broken	,, ,,	
22:26–27	**659, 660**	O Master, let me walk with thee	2 Advent—Friday Proper 7—Thursday	
22:39–46	**171**	Go to dark Gethsemane (st. 1)	3 Advent—Monday Proper 7—Saturday	
22:39–43	**284**	O ye immortal throng (st. 4)	,, ,,	

Lectionary A	Lectionary B	Lectionary C	Pastoral Offices & Episcopal Services	Book of Occasional Services	Lesser Feasts and Fasts
		Proper 28			
		1 Advent			
Maundy Thursday	Maundy Thursday	Maundy Thursday			
,, ,,	,, ,,	,, ,,			
,, ,,	,, ,,	,, ,,			
,, ,,	,, ,,	,, ,,	Ordination: Deacon		
St. Bartholomew	St. Bartholomew	St. Bartholomew			
		Palm Sunday			

			Daily Office Year One	Daily Office Year Two
22:54—23:25	171	Go to dark Gethsemane (st. 2)	3 Advent—Tuesday Proper 8—Monday	
22:54–62	158 231, 232	Ah, holy Jesus, how hast thou offended By all your saints still striving (Confession of Saint Peter)	Proper 8—Monday	
23:11	168, 169 170 598	O sacred head, sore wounded To mock your reign, O dearest Lord Lord Christ, when first thou cam'st to earth	Proper 8—Wednesday	
23:13–25	458	My song is love unknown	Proper 8—Thursday	
23:18–25	158	Ah, holy Jesus, how hast thou offended	,, ,,	
23:26–49	165, 166 168, 169 171	Sing, my tongue, the glorious battle O sacred head, sore wounded Go to dark Gethsemane (st. 3)	Proper 8—Friday	
23:33–56	172	Were you there when they crucified my Lord	Proper 8—Saturday Proper 9—Monday	
23:33–34	240, 241	Hearken to the anthem glorious (st. 3)	Proper 8—Saturday	
23:33	167	There is a green hill far away	,, ,,	
23:34	528	Lord, you give the great commission (st. 4)	,, ,,	
23:39–43	354 356	Into paradise may the angels lead you May choirs of angels lead you	,, ,,	

Lectionary A	Lectionary B	Lectionary C	Pastoral Offices & Episcopal Services	Book of Occasional Services	Lesser Feasts and Fasts
		See Above			
		,, ,,			
		,, ,,			
		,, ,,			
		,, ,,			
		,, ,, Proper 29			
		Palm Sunday			Joseph of Arimathea
		,, ,,			
		,, ,,			
		,, ,,			
		,, ,,			

			Daily Office Year One	Daily Office Year Two
23:42	560	Remember your servants, Lord	See Above	
23:44–46	18	As now the sun shines down at noon	Proper 9—Monday	
23:44	16, 17	Now let us sing our praise to God	,, ,,	
	23	The fleeting day is nearly gone		
	163	Sunset to sunrise changes now		
23:50–56	173	O sorrow deep	,, ,,	
	458	My song is love unknown		
24:1–12	180	He is risen, he is risen	Proper 9—Tuesday	Easter Week—Friday
	183	Christians, to the Paschal victim		
	184	Christ the Lord is risen again		
	190	Lift your voice rejoicing, Mary		
	196, 197	Look there! the Christ, our Brother, comes		
	199, 200	Come, ye faithful, raise the strain		
	201	On earth has dawned this day of days		
	203	O sons and daughters, let us sing (Easter Day)		
	205	Good Christians all, rejoice and sing		
	207	Jesus Christ is risen today		
	208	The strife is o'er, the battle done		
	210	The day of resurrection		
	231, 232	By all your saints still striving (Saint Mary Magdalene)		
	673	The first one ever, oh, ever to know (st. 3)		
24:1	47	On this day, the first of days	,, ,,	,, ,,
	48	O day of radiant gladness		
	50	This is the day the Lord hath made		
	51	We the Lord's people, heart and voice uniting		
	52	This day at thy creating word		
	452	Glorious the day when Christ was born		

Lectionary A	Lectionary B	Lectionary C	Pastoral Offices & Episcopal Services	Book of Occasional Services	Lesser Feasts and Fasts
		See Above			
		,, ,,			
		,, ,,			
		,, ,,			Joseph of Arimathea
		Easter Day—Principal Service			
		,, ,,			

			Daily Office Year One	Daily Office Year Two
24:4–7	284	O ye immortal throng (st. 6)	See Above	See Above
24:13–27, 36–47	180	He is risen, he is risen	Easter Day	Easter Day
	184	Christ the Lord is risen again	Proper 9—Wednesday	
	196, 197	Look there! the Christ, our Brother, comes	Proper 9—Thursday	
	205	Good Christians all, rejoice and sing		
	207	Jesus Christ is risen today		
	208	The strife is o'er, the battle done		
24:28–35	305, 306	Come, risen Lord, and deign to be our guest	Easter Day	,, ,,
	343	Shepherd of souls, refresh and bless	Proper 9—Wednesday	
24:29	662	Abide with me: fast falls the eventide	,, ,,	,, ,,
24:36–43	193	That Easter day with joy was bright	Proper 9—Thursday	
24:50–51	194, 195	Jesus lives! thy terrors now	,, ,,	
	214	Hail the day that sees him rise		
	215	See the Conqueror mounts in triumph		
	217, 218	A hymn of glory let us sing		
	219	The Lord ascendeth up on high		
	220, 221	O Lord Most High, eternal King		
	222	Rejoice, the Lord of life ascends		
	460, 461	Alleluia! sing to Jesus (st. 2)		

Lectionary A	Lectionary B	Lectionary C	Pastoral Offices & Episcopal Services	Book of Occasional Services	Lesser Feasts and Fasts
		See Above			
Easter Day—Evening Service Wednesday in Easter Week Thursday in Easter Week 3 Easter	Easter Day—Evening Service Wednesday in Easter Week Thursday in Easter Week	Easter Day—Evening Service Wednesday in Easter Week Thursday in Easter Week	Ordination: Bishop		Cyril of Jerusalem Boniface William Porcher DuBose Jerome Samuel Isaac Joseph Schereschewsky
,, ,,	,, ,,	,, ,,			,, ,,
,, ,,	,, ,,	,, ,,			,, ,,
	3 Easter		Ordination: Bishop		
Ascension Day	Ascension Day	Ascension Day			Boniface

John:

			Daily Office Year One	Daily Office Year Two
1:1–18	82	Of the Father's love begotten	1 Epiphany—Sunday	1 Epiphany—Monday
	83	O come, all ye faithful (st. 2)	Last Epiphany—Monday	Easter Day
	85, 86	O Savior of our fallen race	Easter Day	Proper 13—Monday
	87	Hark! the herald angels sing (sts. 2 & 3)	Trinity Sunday	Annunciation—Evening Prayer
	88	Sing, O sing, this blessed morn (st. 2)	Annunciation—Evening Prayer	
	102	Once in royal David's city		
	381	Thy strong word did cleave the darkness		
	421	All glory be to God on high		
	443	From God Christ's deity came forth		
	448, 449	O love, how deep, how broad, how high		
	452	Glorious the day when Christ was born		
	489	The great Creator of the worlds		
	491	Where is this stupendous stranger		
	630	Thanks to God whose Word was spoken		
	633	Word of God, come down on earth		
1:1–14	54	Savior of the nations, come	,, ,,	,, ,,
	55	Redeemer of the nations, come		
	371	Thou, whose almighty word		
1:1–4	38, 39	Jesus, Redeemer of the world	,, ,,	,, ,,
1:4–5	649, 650	O Jesus, joy of loving hearts	,, ,,	,, ,,
	692	I heard the voice of Jesus say (st. 3)		
1:6–8	143	The glory of these forty days (st. 3)	,, ,,	,, ,,
1:9	542	Christ is the world's true Light	,, ,,	,, ,,
	692	I heard the voice of Jesus say (st. 3)		
1:14–17	37	O brightness of the immortal Father's face	,, ,,	,, ,,
1:14	365	Come, thou almighty King	,, ,,	,, ,,
	573	Father eternal, Ruler of creation		

Lectionary A	Lectionary B	Lectionary C	Pastoral Offices & Episcopal Services	Book of Occasional Services	Lesser Feasts and Fasts
Christmas Day III 1 Christmas	3 Advent Christmas Day III 1 Christmas	Christmas Day III 1 Christmas		Christmas Festival	
,, ,,	,, ,,	,, ,,		,, ,,	
,, ,,	,, ,,	,, ,,		,, ,,	
,, ,,	,, ,,	,, ,,		,, ,,	
,, ,,	,, ,,	,, ,,		,, ,,	
,, ,,	,, ,,	,, ,,		,, ,,	
,, ,,	,, ,,	,, ,,		,, ,,	
,, ,,	,, ,,	,, ,,		,, ,,	

			Daily Office Year One	Daily Office Year Two
1:15–28	69 70 76	What is the crying at Jordan Herald, sound the note of judgment On Jordan's bank the Baptist's cry		See Above
1:19–36	59	Hark! a thrilling voice is sounding	1 Epiphany—Sunday Last Epiphany—Tuesday	1 Epiphany—Sunday 1 Epiphany—Tuesday Trinity Sunday
1:19–23	67 75	Comfort, comfort ye my people There's a voice in the wilderness crying	,,　　　,,	1 Epiphany—Wednesday Proper 13—Tuesday
1:23	65	Prepare ye the way, O Zion	,,　　　,,	,,　　　,,
1:29–36	307 421	Lord, enthroned in heavenly splendor All glory be to God on high	,,　　　,,	,,　　　,, Proper 13—Wednesday
1:29–35	495	Hail, thou once despised Jesus	,,　　　,, Last Epiphany—Thursday	,,　　　,,
1:29–34	116 120 121 131, 132 135 139 448, 449	"I come," the great Redeemer cries The sinless one to Jordan came Christ, when for us you were baptized When Christ's appearing was made known 　(st. 3) Songs of thankfulness and praise (st. 2) When Jesus went to Jordan's stream O love, how deep, how broad, how high	,,　　　,,	,,　　　,,
1:29	691 693	My faith looks up to thee Just as I am, without one plea	,,　　　,,	,,　　　,,

Lectionary A	Lectionary B	Lectionary C	Pastoral Offices & Episcopal Services	Book of Occasional Services	Lesser Feasts and Fasts
See Above	See Above	See Above		See Above	
	,, ,,				
	,, ,,				
	,, ,,				
2 Epiphany					
,, ,,					
,, ,,					
,, ,,					

			Daily Office Year One	Daily Office Year Two
1:32	509	Spirit divine, attend our prayers	See Above	See Above
	510	Come, Holy Spirit, heavenly Dove		
	512	Come, gracious Spirit, heavenly Dove		
	513	Like the murmur of the dove's song		
1:35–42	231, 232	By all your saints still striving (Saint Andrew)	Last Epiphany—Friday St. Andrew—Evening Prayer	1 Epiphany—Wednesday St. Andrew—Evening Prayer
	549, 550	Jesus calls us; o'er the tumult		
1:40–42	276	For thy blest saints, a noble throng (st. 2)	" "	" "
1:43–46	231, 232	By all your saints still striving (Saint Philip and Saint James)	Last Epiphany—Saturday SS. Philip & James—Morning Prayer St. Bartholomew—Morning Prayer	1 Epiphany—Tuesday Proper 13—Thursday SS. Philip & James—Morning Prayer St. Bartholomew—Morning Prayer
2:1–11	131, 132	When Christ's appearing was made known (st. 4)	January 7 1 Lent—Monday St. Mary the Virgin—Morning Prayer	1 Epiphany—Friday December 29 Proper 13—Friday St. Mary the Virgin—Morning Prayer
	135	Songs of thankfulness and praise (st. 2)		
	138	All praise to you, O Lord		
	443	From God Christ's deity came forth		
3:1–8	295	Sing praise to our Creator	1 Lent—Wednesday	2 Epiphany—Monday Proper 14—Monday
	296	We know that Christ is raised and dies no more		
	297	Descend, O Spirit, purging flame		
3:14–15	473	Lift high the cross	" "	" "
	603, 604	When Christ was lifted from the earth		
3:16–17	489	The great Creator of the worlds (st. 6)	4 Advent—Sunday 1 Lent—Thursday	4 Advent—Sunday 2 Epiphany—Tuesday

Lectionary A	Lectionary B	Lectionary C	Pastoral Offices & Episcopal Services	Book of Occasional Services	Lesser Feasts and Fasts
See Above					
,, ,,					
,, ,,					
	2 Epiphany				
		2 Epiphany			
2 Lent At Baptism	At Baptism	At Baptism		Vigil Before Baptism	2 Easter—Monday
2 Lent					2 Easter—Tuesday
					2 Easter—Wednesday

			Daily Office Year One	Daily Office Year Two
3:16	**421**	All glory be to God on high	See Above	See Above
	530	Spread, O spread, thou mighty word		
4:1–42	**673**	The first one ever, oh, ever to know (st. 2)	2 Epiphany—Sunday 1 Lent—Saturday 2 Lent—Monday	2 Epiphany—Thursday 2 Epiphany—Friday 2 Epiphany—Saturday Proper 14—Wednesday Proper 14—Thursday
4:6	**18**	As now the sun shines down at noon (*Monday and Thursday*)	,, ,,	,, ,,
4:7–15	**327, 328**	Draw nigh and take the Body of the Lord	,, ,,	,, ,,
	522, 523	Glorious things of thee are spoken		
4:13–14	**649, 650**	O Jesus, joy of loving hearts	,, ,,	,, ,,
	692	I heard the voice of Jesus say (st. 2)		
	700	O love that casts out fear		
4:14	**699**	Jesus, Lover of my soul	,, ,,	,, ,,
4:35	**540**	Awake, thou Spirit of the watchmen	,, ,,	,, ,,
	541	Come, labor on		
4:37–38	**289**	Our Father, by whose servants	,, ,,	,, ,,
4:46–54	**493**	O for a thousand tongues to sing	January 8 2 Lent—Tuesday	December 30 3 Epiphany—Monday Proper 14—Friday
	567	Thine arm, O Lord, in days of old		

Lectionary A	Lectionary B	Lectionary C	Pastoral Offices & Episcopal Services	Book of Occasional Services	Lesser Feasts and Fasts
					See Above
3 Lent					3 Lent—Another Proper Dame Julian of Norwich James Otis Sargent Huntington (GC 85)
,, ,,					,, ,,
,, ,,					,, ,,
,, ,,					,, ,,
,, ,,					,, ,,
,, ,, For the Ministry I	For the Ministry I	For the Ministry I			,, ,,
,, ,,	,, ,,	,, ,,			,, ,,
					4 Lent—Monday

			Daily Office Year One	Daily Office Year Two
5:1–18	**135**	Songs of thankfulness and praise (st. 3)	January 9	December 31
	493	O for a thousand tongues to sing	3 Epiphany—Sunday	3 Epiphany—Tuesday
	567	Thine arm, O Lord, in days of old	2 Lent—Wednesday	Proper 14—Saturday
5:43	**50**	This is the day the Lord hath made	4 Advent—Monday	3 Advent—Sunday
	65	Prepare the way, O Zion	2 Lent—Friday	3 Epiphany—Thursday
				Proper 15—Tuesday
6:16–21	**608**	Eternal Father, strong to save	January 11	January 3
			4 Lent—Tuesday	3 Epiphany—Saturday
				Proper 15—Thursday
6:25–69	**301**	Bread of the world, in mercy broken	2 Christmas	2 Christmas
	633	Word of God, come down to earth	January 2	January 7
			January 11	4 Epiphany—Monday
			4 Lent—Wednesday	4 Epiphany—Tuesday
			4 Lent—Thursday	4 Epiphany—Wednesday
			4 Lent—Friday	4 Epiphany—Thursday
			Thanksgiving Day—Morning Prayer	4 Lent—Sunday
				Proper 15—Friday
				Proper 15—Saturday
				Proper 16—Monday
				Proper 16—Tuesday

Lectionary A	Lectionary B	Lectionary C	Pastoral Offices & Episcopal Services	Book of Occasional Services	Lesser Feasts and Fasts
				Public Service of Healing	4 Lent—Tuesday
					4 Lent—Thursday
					2 Easter—Saturday
Of the Holy Eucharist For the Departed	Proper 13 Proper 14 Proper 15 Proper 16 Of the Holy Eucharist For the Departed	Of the Holy Eucharist For the Departed	Ministration to the Sick Burial Ordination: Priest	Public Service of Healing	3 Easter—Monday 3 Easter—Tuesday 3 Easter—Wednesday 3 Easter—Thursday 3 Easter—Friday 3 Easter—Saturday Clement of Alexandria

			Daily Office Year One	Daily Office Year Two
6:25–59	302, 303	Father, we thank thee who has planted	See Above	See Above
	307	Lord, enthroned in heavenly splendor		
	308, 309	O Food to pilgrims given		
	314	Humbly I adore thee, Verity unseen		
	318	Here, O my Lord, I see thee face to face		
	320	Zion, praise thy Savior, singing		
	323	Bread of heaven, on thee we feed		
	327, 328	Draw nigh, and take the Body of the Lord		
	332	O God, unseen yet ever near		
	335	I am the bread of life		
	342	O Bread of life, for sinners broken		
	343	Shepherd of souls, refresh and bless		
	460, 461	Alleluia! sing to Jesus (st. 3)		
	472	Hope of the world, thou Christ of great compassion		
	644	How sweet the Name of Jesus sounds		
	649, 650	O Jesus, joy of loving hearts		
	690	Guide me, O thou great Jehovah		
6:32–59	185, 186	Christ Jesus lay in death's strong bands (st. 4)	,, ,,	,, ,,
6:35	339	Deck thyself, my soul, with gladness	,, ,,	,, ,,
6:37	693	Just as I am, without one plea	,, ,,	,, ,,
	699	Jesus, Lover of my soul		
6:69	421	All glory be to God on high	4 Lent—Saturday	4 Epiphany—Thursday
7:37–38	327, 328	Draw nigh and take the Body of the Lord	December 29	January 8
	649, 650	O Jesus, joy of loving hearts	5 Epiphany—Sunday	5 Epiphany—Monday
	692	I heard the voice of Jesus say (st. 2)	3 Lent—Tuesday	Proper 16—Friday
7:42	443	From God Christ's deity came forth	,, ,,	,, ,,

Lectionary A	Lectionary B	Lectionary C	Pastoral Offices & Episcopal Services	Book of Occasional Services	Lesser Feasts and Fasts
See Above	See Above	See Above	See Above	See Above	See Above
,, ,,	,, ,,	,, ,,	,, ,,	,, ,,	,, ,,
	,, ,,		,, ,,		,, ,,
For the Departed	,, ,,	For the Departed	,, ,,		,, ,,
	,, ,,				3 Easter—Saturday
Day of Pentecost—Early or Vigil Service	Day of Pentecost—Early or Vigili Service	Day of Pentecost—Early or Vigil Service			4 Lent—Saturday
					,, ,,

			Daily Office Year One	Daily Office Year Two
8:12	6, 7	Christ, whose glory fills the skies	December 31	January 9
	490	I want to walk as a child of the light	6 Epiphany—Sunday	5 Epiphany—Wednesday
	542	Christ is the world's true Light	3 Lent—Wednesday	Proper 10—Saturday
	672	O very God of very God		
	692	I heard the voice of Jesus say (st. 3)		
8:32	419	Lord of all being, throned afar	3 Lent—Thursday	5 Epiphany—Thursday
			The Presentation—Morning Prayer	Proper 17—Monday
				The Presentation—Morning Prayer
8:58	401	The God of Abraham praise	3 Lent—Saturday	5 Epiphany—Saturday
	439	What wondrous love is this		5 Lent—Sunday
				Proper 17—Wednesday
9:1–41	371	Thou, whose almighty Word	January 12	January 4
	493	O for a thousand tongues to sing	5 Lent—Monday	6 Epiphany—Monday
	567	Thine arm, O Lord, in days of old	5 Lent—Tuesday	6 Epiphany—Tuesday
	633	Word of God, come down on earth		Proper 17—Thursday
				Proper 17—Friday
9:4	570, 571	All who love and serve your city	,, ,,	,, ,,
9:5	692	I heard the voice of Jesus say (st. 3)	,, ,,	,, ,,
10:1–30	478	Jesus, our mighty Lord	January 3	January 10
	645, 646	The King of love my shepherd is	7 Epiphany—Sunday	6 Epiphany—Wednesday
			5 Lent—Wednesday	6 Epiphany—Thursday
			5 Lent—Thursday	Proper 17—Saturday
				Proper 18—Monday
10:1–18	708	Savior, like a shepherd lead us	,, ,,	,, ,,
10:14–16	334	Praise the Lord, rise up rejoicing	,, ,,	,, ,,

Lectionary A	Lectionary B	Lectionary C	Pastoral Offices & Episcopal Services	Book of Occasional Services	Lesser Feasts and Fasts
					5 Lent—Monday
					5 Lent—Wednesday Gregory of Nazianzus
					5 Lent—Thursday
4 Lent				Public Service of Healing	4 Lent—Another Proper
,, ,,				,, ,,	,, ,,
,, ,,				,, ,,	,, ,,
4 Easter	4 Easter	4 Easter	Burial Ordination: Priest	Burial	4 Easter—Monday 4 Easter—Tuesday Timothy and Titus Cyprian
,, ,,	,, ,,		,, ,,	,, ,,	,, ,,
	,, ,,		,, ,,	,, ,,	,, ,,

			Daily Office Year One	Daily Office Year Two
10:15	205	Good Christians all, rejoice and sing (st. 4)	See Above	See Above
	304	I come with joy to meet my Lord		
11:1–44	493	O for a thousand tongues to sing	5 Lent—Friday	January 5
	567	Thine arm, O Lord, in days of old	5 Lent—Saturday	6 Epiphany—Saturday
				7 Epiphany—Monday
				7 Epiphany—Tuesday
				7 Epiphany—Wednesday
				7 Epiphany—Thursday
				7 Epiphany—Friday
11:14–16	242	How oft, O Lord, thy face hath shone	,, ,,	,, ,,
11:25–27	335	I am the bread of life	,, ,,	,, ,,
11:35	715	When Jesus wept, the falling tear	,, ,,	,, ,,
12:12–19	486	Hosanna to the living Lord	Holy Week—Monday	7 Epiphany—Friday
				Proper 19—Tuesday
12:12–15	50	This is the day the Lord hath made (sts. 3–5)	,, ,,	,, ,,
	65	Prepare the way, O Zion		
	71, 72	Hark! the glad sound! the Savior comes (st. 4)		
	74	Blest be the King whose coming		
	104	A stable lamp is lighted (st. 2)		
	154, 155	All glory, laud, and honor		
	156	Ride on! ride on in majesty		
	458	My song is love unknown		
	480	When Jesus left his Father's throne		
12:20–22	231, 232	By all your saints still striving (Saint Philip and Saint James)	Holy Week—Tuesday	7 Epiphany—Saturday
			SS. Philip & James—Evening Prayer	Proper 19—Wednesday
				SS. Philip & James—Evening Prayer

Lectionary A	Lectionary B	Lectionary C	Pastoral Offices & Episcopal Services	Book of Occasional Services	Lesser Feasts and Fasts
	See Above		See Above	See Above	See Above
5 Lent For the Departed	For the Departed	For the Departed	Burial	Celebration for a Home	5 Lent—Another Proper
,, ,,					
,, ,,	,, ,,	,, ,,	,, ,,		,, ,,
,, ,,					,, ,,
	5 Lent				

			Daily Office Year One	Daily Office Year Two
12:24	**204**	Now the green blade riseth	See Above Last Epiphany—Saturday	See Above
12:26	**655**	O Jesus, I have promised	,, ,,	,, ,,
12:32–36	**473**	Lift high the cross	Last Epiphany—Saturday Holy Week—Wednesday The Transfiguration—Evening Prayer	8 Epiphany—Monday Proper 19—Thursday The Transfiguration—Evening Pray
12:32–33	**603, 604**	When Christ was lifted from the earth	,, ,,	,, ,,
12:35–36, 46	**490**	I want to walk as a child of the Light	5 Lent—Saturday	,, ,,
12:35–36	**692**	I heard the voice of Jesus say (st. 3)	,, ,,	,, ,,
12:46	**6, 7** **672** **692**	Christ, whose glory fills the skies O very God of very God I heard the voice of Jesus say (st. 3)	,, ,,	8 Epiphany—Tuesday 1 Lent—Sunday Proper 19—Saturday
13:1–17	**602**	Jesu, Jesu, fill us with your love		8 Epiphany—Wednesday
14:1–3	**194, 195**	Jesus lives! thy terrors now	Easter Week—Monday 2 Easter—Sunday St. Thomas—Evening Prayer	8 Epiphany—Saturday 2 Easter—Sunday 2 Easter—Monday St. Thomas—Evening Prayer

Lectionary A	Lectionary B	Lectionary C	Pastoral Offices & Episcopal Services	Book of Occasional Services	Lesser Feasts and Fasts
Of the Holy Cross	5 Lent Of the Holy Cross	Of the Holy Cross		Rogation Procession	Laurence Constance and her Companions (GC 85) Ignatius
,, ,,	,, ,,	,, ,,		,, ,,	,, ,,
,, ,, Holy Cross	,, ,, Holy Cross	,, ,, Holy Cross			
,, ,,	,, ,,	,, ,,			
,, ,, Tuesday in Holy Week	,, ,, Tuesday in Holy Week	,, ,, Tuesday in Holy Week			Justin William Tyndale
					4 Easter—Wednesday
Tuesday in Holy Week	Tuesday in Holy Week	Tuesday in Holy Week			Justin William Tyndale
Maundy Thursday	Maundy Thursday	Maundy Thursday			
5 Easter			Burial		4 Easter—Friday Remigius

			Daily Office Year One	Daily Office Year Two
14:2–3	1, 2	Father, we praise thee, now the night is over	See Above	See Above
	484, 485	Praise the Lord through every nation		
14:5–9	490	I want to walk as a child of the Light (st. 2)	" " January 4	" " January 11
14:6	457	Thou art the Way, to thee alone	" "	" "
	463, 464	He is the Way		
	478	Jesus, our mighty Lord		
	487	Come, my Way, my Truth, my Life		
	644	How sweet the Name of Jesus sounds		
	703	Lead us, O Father, in the paths of peace		
14:13–14	248, 249	To the Name of our salvation	" "	" "
	518	Christ is made the sure foundation		
	711	Seek ye first the kingdom of God		
14:16	226, 227	Come, thou Holy Spirit bright	Easter Week—Tuesday	2 Easter—Monday
	228	Holy Spirit, font of light	SS. Simon & Jude—Evening Prayer	SS. Simon & Jude—Evening Prayer
	500	Creator Spirit, by whose aid		
	514	To thee, O Comforter divine		
	516	Come down, O Love divine		
14:26	226, 227	Come, thou Holy Spirit bright	Easter Week—Tuesday	2 Easter—Tuesday
	228	Holy Spirit, font of light	Day of Pentecost	SS. Simon & Jude—Evening Prayer
	500	Creator Spirit, by whose aid	SS. Simon & Jude—Evening Prayer	
	514	To thee, O Comforter divine		
15:1–11	513	Like the murmur of the dove's song	January 5 Easter Week—Wednesday	January 12 2 Easter—Wednesday

Lectionary A	Lectionary B	Lectionary C	Pastoral Offices & Episcopal Services	Book of Occasional Services	Lesser Feasts and Fasts
See Above			See Above		See Above
,, ,, Day of Pentecost— Principal Service SS. Philip & James	Day of Pentecost— Principal Service SS. Philip & James	Day of Pentecost— Principal Service SS. Philip & James	,, ,,		,, ,, Augustine of Hippo
,, ,,	,, ,,	,, ,,	,, ,,		,, ,,
,, ,,	,, ,,	,, ,,	New Ministry		4 Easter—Saturday Augustine of Hippo
,, ,, At Confirmation	,, ,, 5 Easter At Confirmation	,, ,, At Confirmation			
		6 Easter			5 Easter—Monday Gregory of Nyssa
6 Easter St. Matthias For a Church Convention	6 Easter St. Matthias For a Church Convention	St. Matthias For a Church Convention	Marriage New Ministry		5 Easter—Wednesday 5 Easter—Thursday Aelred (GC 85) Wulfstan Bernard

			Daily Office Year One	Daily Office Year Two
15:1–8, 16	**344** **392**	Lord, dismiss us with thy blessing Come, we that love the Lord	See Above	See Above
15:1–6	**198** **323**	Thou hallowed chosen morn of praise Bread of heaven, on thee we feed	,, ,,	,, ,,
15:7	**518**	Christ is made the sure foundation	,, ,,	,, ,,
15:13	**319** **458**	You, Lord, we praise in songs of celebration My song is love unknown	,, ,,	,, ,, 2 Easter—Thursday
15:14–16	**348**	Lord, we have come at your own invitation	,, ,,	,, ,,
15:16	**706**	In your mercy, Lord, you called me	,, ,,	,, ,,
15:16b	**518**	Christ is made the sure foundation	,, ,,	,, ,,
15:26–27	**514**	To thee, O Comforter divine	Easter Week—Thursday	,, ,,
15:26	**365**	Come, thou almighty King	,, ,,	,, ,,
16:13–15	**512**	Come, gracious Spirit, heavenly Dove	Easter Week—Friday	2 Easter—Friday
16:23	**711**	Seek ye first the kingdom of God	Holy Name Easter Week—Saturday	2 Easter—Saturday

Lectionary A	Lectionary B	Lectionary C	Pastoral Offices & Episcopal Services	Book of Occasional Services	Lesser Feasts and Fasts
See Above	See Above	See Above	New Ministry		See Above
,, ,,	,, ,,	,, ,,			,, ,,
,, ,,	,, ,,	,, ,,			,, ,,
,, ,,	,, ,,	,, ,,	New Ministry		,, ,, Absalom Jones
,, ,,	,, ,,	,, ,,	,, ,,		5 Easter—Friday Absalom Jones
,, ,,	,, ,,	,, ,,	,, ,,		,, ,,
,, ,,	,, ,,	,, ,,	,, ,,		,, ,,
SS. Simon & Jude	SS. Simon & Jude	SS. Simon & Jude			6 Easter—Monday Latimer, Ridley, and Cranmer
,, ,,	,, ,,	,, ,,			,, ,,
		Trinity Sunday			6 Easter—Wednesday
For Peace	For Peace	For Peace			6 Easter—Friday 6 Easter—Saturday Monnica

			Daily Office Year One	Daily Office Year Two
17:1–26	315	Thou, who at thy first Eucharist didst pray	Maundy Thursday 2 Easter—Monday 2 Easter—Tuesday 2 Easter—Wednesday	Last Epiphany—Thursday Last Epiphany—Friday Last Epiphany—Saturday
17:20–23	305, 306	Come, risen Lord, and deign to be our guest	,, ,,	Last Epiphany—Monday
18:12—19:16	171	Go to dark Gethsemane (st. 2)		,, ,,
18:15–27	158 231, 232	Ah, holy Jesus, how hast thou offended By all your saints still striving (Confession of Saint Peter)		Last Epiphany—Tuesday
18:28—19:16	458	My song is love unknown		
18:39–40	158	Ah, holy Jesus, how hast thou offended		
19:2–5	168, 169 170 598	O sacred head, sore wounded To mock your reign, O dearest Lord Lord Christ, when first thou cam'st to earth		
19:17–42	172	Were you there when they crucified my Lord	Good Friday St. Mary the Virgin—Evening Prayer	Good Friday St. Mary the Virgin—Evening Prayer

Lectionary A	Lectionary B	Lectionary C	Pastoral Offices & Episcopal Services	Book of Occasional Services	Lesser Feasts and Fasts
7 Easter Of a Theologian and Teacher I For the Unity of the Church	7 Easter Of a Theologian and Teacher I For the Unity of the Church	7 Easter Of a Theologian and Teacher I For the Unity of the Church	Ordination: Bishop		7 Easter—Tuesday 7 Easter—Wednesday 7 Easter—Thursday William Reed Huntington John Henry Hobart Richard Hooker
,, ,,	,, ,,	,, ,,	,, ,,		,, ,,
Good Friday	Good Friday	Good Friday			Frederick Denison Maurice
,, ,,	,, ,,	,, ,,			
,, ,, Of the Reign of Christ	,, ,, Of the Reign of Christ	,, ,, Of the Reign of Christ			,, ,,
Good Friday	Good Friday	Good Friday			
,, ,,	,, ,,	,, ,,			
,, ,,	,, ,,	,, ,,			

			Daily Office Year One	Daily Office Year Two
19:17–37	**165, 166** **168, 169** **171**	Sing, my tongue, the glorious battle O sacred head, sore wounded Go to dark Gethsemane (st. 3)	St. Mary the Virgin—Evening Prayer	St. Mary the Virgin—Evening Praye
19:17–18	**167**	There is a green hill far away		
19:25–27	**278**	Sing we of the blessed Mother	,, ,,	,, ,,
19:25	**159**	At the cross her vigil keeping	,, ,,	,, ,,
19:30	**23**	The fleeting day is nearly gone		
19:34	**161** **307** **308, 309** **685**	The flaming banners of our King (st. 2) Lord, enthroned in heavenly splendor O Food to pilgrims given Rock of ages, cleft for me		
19:38–42	**173** **458**	O sorrow deep My song is love unknown	Good Friday	Good Friday
20:1–23	**199, 200** **203**	Come, ye faithful, raise the strain O sons and daughters, let us sing (Easter Day)	Easter Day	Easter Day

Lectionary A	Lectionary B	Lectionary C	Pastoral Offices & Episcopal Services	Book of Occasional Services	Lesser Feasts and Fasts
See Above	See Above	See Above			
,, ,,	,, ,,	,, ,,			
,, ,,	,, ,,	,, ,,			
,, ,,	,, ,,	,, ,,			
,, ,,	,, ,,	,, ,,			
,, ,,	,, ,,	,, ,,			
Holy Saturday	Holy Saturday	Holy Saturday			
Easter Day—Principal Service Tuesday in Easter Week St. Mary Magdalene	Tuesday in Easter Week St. Mary Magdalene	Tuesday in Easter Week St. Mary Magdalene	Ordination: Bishop		

			Daily Office Year One		Daily Office Year Two	
20:1–18	180	He is risen, he is risen				
	183	Christians, to the Paschal victim				
	184	Christ the Lord is risen again				
	190	Lift your voice rejoicing, Mary				
	196, 197	Look there! the Christ, our Brother, comes				
	201	On earth has dawned this day of days				
	205	Good Christians all, rejoice and sing				
	207	Jesus Christ is risen today				
	208	The strife is o'er, the battle done				
	210	The day of resurrection				
	231, 232	By all your saints still striving (Saint Mary Magdalene)				
	673	The first one ever, oh, ever to know (st. 3)				
20:1	47	On this day, the first of days				
	48	O day of radiant gladness				
	50	This is the day the Lord hath made				
	51	We the Lord's people, heart and voice uniting				
	52	This day at thy creating word				
	452	Glorious the day when Christ was born				
20:19–31	193	That Easter day with joy was bright	"	"	"	"
	206	O sons and daughters, let us sing (Second Sunday of Easter and Saint Thomas' Day)				
	209	We walk by faith, and not by sight				
	212	Awake, arise, lift up your voice				
20:22–23	511	Holy Spirit, ever living	"	"	"	"
20:22	508	Breathe on me, Breath of God	"	"	"	"
20:24–29	57, 58	Lo! he comes, with clouds descending				
	231, 232	By all your saints still striving (Saint Thomas)				
	242	How oft, O Lord, thy face hath shone				

Lectionary A	Lectionary B	Lectionary C	Pastoral Offices & Episcopal Services	Book of Occasional Services	Lesser Feasts and Fasts
See Above	See Above	See Above			
Easter Day—Principal Service					

2 Easter
Day of Pentecost—
  Principal Service
St. Thomas
	2 Easter
	Day of Pentecost—
	  Principal Service
	St. Thomas
		2 Easter
		Day of Pentecost—
		  Principal Service
		St. Thomas
			Ordination: Bishop		

,, ,,	,, ,,	,, ,,	,, ,,		
,, ,,	,, ,,	,, ,,	,, ,,		
,, ,,	,, ,,	,, ,,			

			Daily Office Year One	Daily Office Year Two
21:15–17	231, 232	By all your saints still striving (Confession of Saint Peter)	3 Easter—Sunday Confession of St. Peter—Evening Prayer	Confession of St. Peter—Evening Prayer
21:24	231, 232 245	By all your saints still striving (Saint John) Praise God for John, evangelist		

Acts:

			Daily Office Year One	Daily Office Year Two
1:1–11	214 215 217, 218 219 220, 221 222 460, 461	Hail the day that sees him rise See the Conqueror mounts in triumph A hymn of glory let us sing The Lord ascendeth up on high O Lord Most High, eternal King Rejoice, the Lord of life ascends Alleluia! sing to Jesus (st. 2)	Proper 6—Monday St. Mary the Virgin—Evening Prayer St. Luke—Evening Prayer	Proper 12—Wednesday St. Mary the Virgin—Evening Prayer St. Luke—Evening Prayer
1:1–3	285	What thanks and praise to thee we owe	Proper 6—Monday St. Luke—Evening Prayer	Proper 12—Wednesday St. Luke—Evening Prayer
1:8	501, 502 506, 507 513 521 531 539	O Holy Spirit, by whose breath Praise the Spirit in creation Like the murmur of the dove's song Put forth, O God, thy Spirit's might O Spirit of the living God O Zion, haste, thy mission high fulfilling	Proper 6—Monday St. Mary the Virgin—Evening Prayer St. Luke—Evening Prayer	Proper 12—Wednesday St. Mary the Virgin—Evening Prayer St. Luke—Evening Prayer
1:9	194, 195	Jesus lives! thy terrors now	Proper 6—Monday St. Mary the Virgin—Evening Prayer	Proper 12—Wednesday St. Mary the Virgin—Evening Prayer

Lectionary A	Lectionary B	Lectionary C	Pastoral Offices & Episcopal Services	Book of Occasional Services	Lesser Feasts and Fasts
SS. Peter & Paul Of a Pastor I	SS. Peter & Paul Of a Pastor I	SS. Peter & Paul Of a Pastor I			7 Easter—Friday William White Charles Simeon
St. John	St. John	St. John			7 Easter—Saturday
Ascension Day 7 Easter Of a Missionary I	Ascension Day Of a Missionary I	Ascension Day Of a Missionary I			Channing Moore Williams Anskar Willibrord
,, ,,	,, ,,	,, ,,			,, ,,
,, ,,	,, ,,	,, ,,			,, ,,
,, ,,	,, ,,	,, ,,			,, ,,

			Daily Office Year One	Daily Office Year Two
1:10–11	284	O ye immortal throng (st. 7)	See Above	See Above
1:11	435	At the Name of Jesus	,, ,,	,, ,,
1:12–14	278	Sing we of the blessed Mother	,, ,,	,, ,,
1:15–26	231, 232	By all your saints still striving (Saint Matthias)	Proper 6—Tuesday	Proper 12—Thursday
2:1–42	223, 224	Hail this joyful day's return	Easter Week—Monday	Proper 12—Friday
	225	Hail thee, festival day (Pentecost)	Easter Week—Tuesday	Proper 12—Saturday
	229	Spirit of mercy, truth, and love	Proper 6—Wednesday	Proper 13—Monday
	230	A mighty sound from heaven	Proper 6—Thursday	
	297	Descend, O Spirit, purging flame	Proper 6—Friday	
	299	Spirit of God, unleashed on earth		
2:1–11	506, 507	Praise the Spirit in creation	Proper 6—Wednesday	Proper 12—Friday
2:1–4	531	O Spirit of the living God	,, ,,	,, ,,
2:1–3	226, 227	Come, thou holy Spirit bright	,, ,,	,, ,,
	228	Holy Spirit, font of light		
	500	Creator Spirit, by whose aid		
	501, 502	O Holy Spirit, by whose breath		
	503, 504	Come, Holy Ghost, our souls inspire		
	509	Spirit divine, attend our prayers		
	513	Like the murmur of the dove's song		
	704	O thou who camest from above		
2:1–2	579	Almighty Father, strong to save	,, ,,	,, ,,

Lectionary A	Lectionary B	Lectionary C	Pastoral Offices & Episcopal Services	Book of Occasional Services	Lesser Feasts and Fasts
Ascension Day 7 Easter	Ascension Day	Ascension Day			
,, ,,	,, ,,	,, ,,			
7 Easter					
St. Matthias	7 Easter St. Matthias	St. Matthias			
Monday in Easter Week Tuesday in Easter Week 2 Easter 3 Easter Day of Pentecost	Monday in Easter Week Tuesday in Easter Week Day of Pentecost	Monday in Easter Week Tuesday in Easter Week Day of Pentecost		Special Vocation	The First Book of Common Prayer
Day of Pentecost	Day of Pentecost	Day of Pentecost			
,, ,,	,, ,,	,, ,,			
,, ,,	,, ,,	,, ,,			
,, ,,	,, ,,	,, ,,			

			Daily Office Year One	Daily Office Year Two
2:1	47	On this day, the first of days	See Above	See Above
	48	O day of radiant gladness		
	51	We the Lord's people, heart and voice uniting		
	52	This day at thy creating word		
2:15	12, 13	The golden sun lights up the sky	,, ,,	,, ,,
2:21	248, 249	To the Name of our salvation	,, ,,	,, ,,
	252	Jesus! Name of wondrous love		
	435	At the Name of Jesus		
2:22–36	184	Christ the Lord is risen again	Easter Week—Monday	Proper 12—Saturday
	192	This joyful Eastertide	Easter Week—Tuesday	
	215	See the Conqueror mounts in triumph	Proper 6—Thursday	
	455, 456	O love of God, how strong and true		
	492	Sing, ye faithful, sing with gladness		
2:32–33	364	O God, we praise thee, and confess	Easter Week—Monday	,, ,,
	366	Holy God, we praise thy Name	Proper 6—Thursday	
	421	All glory be to God on high		
2:36	483	The head that once was crowned with thorns	Easter Week—Tuesday	,, ,,
			Proper 6—Thursday	
3:1–10	23	The fleeting day is nearly gone	Easter Week—Wednesday	Proper 13—Tuesday
3:12–26	492	Sing, ye faithful, sing with gladness	Easter Week—Thursday	Proper 13—Wednesday

206   *Acts*

Lectionary A	Lectionary B	Lectionary C	Pastoral Offices & Episcopal Services	Book of Occasional Services	Lesser Feasts and Fasts
See Above	See Above	See Above			
Monday in Easter Week Tuesday in Easter Week 2 Easter	Monday in Easter Week Tuesday in Easter Week	Monday in Easter Week Tuesday in Easter Week			
Monday in Easter Week	Monday in Easter Week	Monday in Easter Week			
Tuesday in Easter Week 3 Easter	Tuesday in Easter Week	Tuesday in Easter Week			
Wednesday in Easter Week	Wednesday in Easter Week	Wednesday in Easter Week		Public Service of Healing	
Thursday in Easter Week	Thursday in Easter Week 2 Easter	Thursday in Easter Week			

			Daily Office Year One	Daily Office Year Two
4:7–12	**248, 249**	To the Name of our salvation	Easter Week—Friday	Proper 13—Thursday
	252	Jesus! Name of wondrous love	The Patronal Feast	The Patronal Feast
4:11–12	**518**	Christ is made the sure foundation	,, ,,	,, ,,
	525	The Church's one foundation		
4:12	**435**	At the Name of Jesus	,, ,,	,, ,,
4:36–37	**231, 232**	By all your saints still striving (Saint Barnabas)	Proper 6—Saturday St. Barnabas—Morning Prayer	Proper 13—Saturday St. Barnabas—Morning Prayer
5:30–31	**364**	O God, we praise thee, and confess	Proper 7—Tuesday	Proper 14—Tuesday
	366	Holy God, we praise thy Name		
	421	All glory be to God on high		
	483	The head that once was crowned with thorns		
6:1—8:2	**243**	When Stephen, full of power and grace	Proper 7—Wednesday Proper 7—Thursday Proper 7—Friday Proper 7—Saturday Proper 8—Monday St. Stephen	Proper 14—Wednesday Proper 14—Thursday Proper 14—Friday Proper 14—Saturday Proper 15—Monday St. Stephen
7:32	**401**	The God of Abraham praise	Proper 8—Saturday	Proper 14—Saturday
7:54–60	**231, 232**	By all your saints still striving (Saint Stephen)	Proper 8—Monday St. Stephen—Evening Prayer	Proper 15—Monday St. Stephen—Evening Payer
	237	Let us now our voices raise (st. 2)		

Lectionary A	Lectionary B	Lectionary C	Pastoral Offices & Episcopal Services	Book of Occasional Services	Lesser Feasts and Fasts
Friday in Easter Week Confession of St. Peter	Friday in Easter Week 3 Easter Confession of St. Peter	Friday in Easter Week Confession of St. Peter			
,, ,,	,, ,,	,, ,,			
,, ,,	,, ,,	,, ,,			
	4 Easter				2 Easter—Tuesday
Easter Day—Evening Service	Easter Day—Evening Service	Easter Day—Evening Service			2 Easter—Thursday
4 Easter St. Stephen	St. Stephen	St. Stephen	Ordination: Deacon		2 Easter—Saturday 3 Easter—Monday 3 Easter—Tuesday
,, ,,	,, ,,	,, ,,			3 Easter—Tuesday

			Daily Office Year One	Daily Office Year Two
7:55–56	364 366 421	O God, we praise thee, and confess Holy God, we praise thy Name All glory be to God on high	See Above	See Above
7:59–60	240, 241	Hearken to the anthem glorious (st. 2)	,, ,,	,, ,,
8:26–40	297	Descend, O Spirit, purging flame	Proper 8—Thursday	Proper 4—Sunday Proper 15—Thursday
9:1–22	255 256 231, 232	We sing the glorious conquest A light from heaven shone round By all your saints still striving (Conversion of Saint Paul)	Proper 8—Friday Proper 8—Saturday Proper 20—Sunday Conversion of St. Paul—Evening Prayer	Proper 15—Friday Proper 15—Saturday Proper 16—Monday Conversion of St. Paul—Evening Prayer
9:3–8	18	As now the sun shines down at noon (*Tuesday and Saturday*)	Proper 8—Friday Conversion of St. Paul—Evening Prayer	Proper 15—Friday Conversion of St. Paul—Evening Prayer
10:9	18	As now the sun shines down at noon (*Wednesday and Friday*)	Proper 9—Wednesday	Proper 5—Sunday Proper 16—Wednesday
10:39–40	175 179 216	Hail thee, festival day (Easter) "Welcome, happy morning!" age to age shall say Hail thee, festival day (Ascension)	Proper 9—Friday Confession of St. Peter—Morning Prayer	Proper 16—Friday Confession of St. Peter—Morning Prayer
10:42	63, 64 364 366 421	O heavenly Word, eternal light O God, we praise thee, and confess Holy God, we praise thy Name All glory be to God on high	,, ,,	,, ,,
10:44–48	297	Descend, O Spirit, purging flame	,, ,,	,, ,,

Lectionary A	Lectionary B	Lectionary C	Pastoral Offices & Episcopal Services	Book of Occasional Services	Lesser Feasts and Fasts
See Above	See Above	See Above			See Above
,, ,,	,, ,,	,, ,,			,, ,,
	5 Easter				3 Easter—Thursday
		3 Easter			3 Easter—Friday
		,, ,,			,, ,,
Easter Day—Principal Service	Easter Day—Principal Service	Easter Day—Principal Service		Public Service of Healing	
,, ,,	,, ,,	,, ,,		,, ,,	
					3 Easter—Saturday

			Daily Office Year One	Daily Office Year Two
12:1–2	**231, 232**	By all your saints still striving (Saint James)	Proper 10—Tuesday Proper 22—Sunday	Proper 17—Tuesday
	276	For thy blest saints, a noble throng		
12:25	**231, 232**	By all your saints still striving (Saint Mark)	Proper 10—Wednesday St. Mark—Morning Prayer	Proper 17—Wednesday St. Mark—Morning Prayer
13:52	**515**	Holy Ghost, dispel our sadness	Proper 11—Monday	Proper 18—Monday
15:34	**231, 232**	By all your saints still striving (Saint James of Jerusalem)	Proper 11—Saturday	Proper 18—Saturday
15:36–40	**231, 232**	By all your saints still striving (Saint Mark)	Proper 12—Monday	Proper 19—Monday
17:6	**506, 507**	Praise the Spirit in creation	Proper 12—Friday	Proper 19—Friday
20:28	**40, 41**	O Christ, you are both light and day	Proper 14—Monday	Proper 21—Monday
	525	The Church's one foundation	St. Matthias—Evening Prayer	St. Matthias—Evening Prayer
22:1–16	**231, 232**	By all your saints still striving (Conversion of Saint Paul)	Proper 14—Friday	Proper 21—Friday
	255	We sing the glorious conquest		
	256	A light from heaven shone around		
22:6	**18**	As now the sun shines down at noon (*Tuesday and Saturday*)	,, ,,	,, ,,

Lectionary A	Lectionary B	Lectionary C	Pastoral Offices & Episcopal Services	Book of Occasional Services	Lesser Feasts and Fasts
St. James	St. James	St. James			
					4 Easter—Wednesday
		5 Easter			4 Easter—Saturday
5 Easter					
Of a Pastor II	Of a Pastor II	Of a Pastor II			7 Easter—Wednesday Boniface Robert Grosseteste Consecration of Samuel Seabury

			Daily Office Year One	Daily Office Year Two
26:9–21	**231, 232**	By all your saints still striving (Conversion of Saint Paul)	Proper 16—Monday	Proper 23—Monday
	255	We sing the glorious conquest		
	256	A light from heaven shone around		
26:13	**18**	As now the sun shines down at noon (*Tuesday and Saturday*)	,, ,,	,, ,,

Romans:

			Daily Office Year One	Daily Office Year Two
2:16	**63, 64**	O heavenly Word, eternal Light	2 Lent—Thursday	Proper 6—Thursday
3:10–26	**151**	From deepest woe I cry to thee	2 Lent—Friday 2 Lent—Saturday	Proper 6—Saturday Proper 7—Monday
3:23–25a	**495**	Hail, thou once despised Jesus	2 Lent—Saturday	Proper 7—Monday
3:23–24	**671**	Amazing grace! how sweet the sound	,, ,,	,, ,,
	686	Come, thou fount of every blessing		
5:2	**686**	Come, thou fount of every blessing	3 Lent—Wednesday Proper 9—Sunday	Proper 7—Thursday
5:5	**226, 227**	Come, thou Holy Spirit bright	,, ,,	,, ,,
	500	Creator Spirit, by whose aid		
	510	Come, Holy Spirit, heavenly Dove		
	516	Come down, O Love divine		

Lectionary A	Lectionary B	Lectionary C	Pastoral Offices & Episcopal Services	Book of Occasional Services	Lesser Feasts and Fasts
Conversion of St. Paul	Conversion of St. Paul	Conversion of St. Paul			
,, ,,	,, ,,	,, ,,			
Proper 4					
,, ,,					
,, ,,					
3 Lent					Anselm
,, ,,					,, ,,

			Daily Office Year One	Daily Office Year Two
5:6–11	**167**	There is a green hill far away	See Above	See Above
5:8–11	**458**	My song is love unknown	,, ,,	,, ,,
5:8–10	**455, 456**	O love of God, how strong and true	,, ,,	,, ,,
5:12–21	**60** **176, 177** **270** **295** **445, 446**	Creator of the stars of night Over the chaos of the empty waters Gabriel's message does away Sing praise to our Creator Praise to the Holiest in the height	3 Lent—Thursday Eve of the Annunciation	Proper 7—Friday Eve of the Annunciation
5:15–17	**686**	Come, thou fount of every blessing	,, ,,	,, ,,
5:18–21	**671**	Amazing grace! how sweet the sound	,, ,,	,, ,,
6:2–11	**149**	Eternal Lord of love, behold your Church	3 Lent—Friday	2 Lent—Sunday Proper 7—Saturday
6:3–11	**47** **187** **294** **296** **298**	On this day, the first of days Through the Red Sea brought at last Baptized in water We know that Christ is raised and dies no more All who believe and are baptized	,, ,,	,, ,,

Lectionary A	Lectionary B	Lectionary C	Pastoral Offices & Episcopal Services	Book of Occasional Services	Lesser Feasts and Fasts
See Above Proper 6					See Above
,, ,,					,, ,,
,, ,,					,, ,,
1 Lent Proper 7					
,, ,,					
,, ,,					
Easter Day—Vigil or 　Early Service Proper 8 For All Baptized 　Christians At Baptism	Easter Day—Vigil or 　Early Service For All Baptized 　Christians At Baptism	Easter Day—Vigil or 　Early Service For All Baptized 　Christians At Baptism		Vigil Before Baptism	
,, ,,	,, ,,	,, ,,		,, ,,	

			Daily Office Year One	Daily Office Year Two
6:6–11	**697**	My God, accept my heart this day	See Above	See Above
6:9–10	**183** **205**	Christians, to the Paschal victim Good Christians all, rejoice and sing (st. 4)	,, ,,	,, ,,
6:15–23	**252**	Jesus! Name of wondrous love (st. 5)	3 Lent—Saturday	Proper 8—Monday
6:16–23	**60** **270**	Creator of the stars of night Gabriel's message does away	,, ,,	,, ,,
8:18	**621, 622** **623**	Light's abode, celestial Salem O what their joy and their glory must be	4 Lent—Thursday Eve of the Presentation	4 Lent—Sunday Proper 8—Saturday Eve of the Presentation
8:19–23	**60**	Creator of the stars of night	,, ,,	,, ,,
8:26–27	**698** **513**	Eternal Spirit of the living Christ Like the murmur of the dove's song	,, ,,	Proper 9—Monday
8:28	**677**	God moves in a mysterious way	4 Lent—Friday	,, ,,
8:32	**530**	Spread, O spread, thou mighty word	,, ,,	Proper 9—Tuesday

Lectionary A	Lectionary B	Lectionary C	Pastoral Offices & Episcopal Services	Book of Occasional Services	Lesser Feasts and Fasts
Easter Day—Vigil or Early Service Proper 8 For All Baptized Christians	Easter Day—Vigil or Early Service For All Baptized Christians	Easter Day—Vigil or Early Service For All Baptized Christians			
,, ,,	,, ,,	,, ,,			
5 Lent					
,, ,,					
Proper 11 At Confirmation For Rogation Days I	At Confirmation For Rogation Days I	At Confirmation For Rogation Days I	Burial	Public Service of Healing	
Day of Pentecost—Early or Vigil Service Proper 11 At Confirmation For Rogation Days I	Day of Pentecost—Early or Vigil Service At Confirmation For Rogation Days I	Day of Pentecost—Early or Vigil Service At Confirmation For Rogation Days I	,, ,,	,, ,,	
Day of Pentecost—Early or Vigil Service Proper 12 At Confirmation	Day of Pentecost—Early or Vigil Service At Confirmation	Day of Pentecost—Early or Vigil Service At Confirmation			
Proper 12					
,, ,,	2 Lent			Public Service of Healing	

			Daily Office Year One	Daily Office Year Two
8:34–39	194, 195 447	Jesus lives! thy terrors now The Christ who died but rose again	See Above	See Above
8:34	364 366 421 460, 461 495	O God, we praise thee, and confess Holy God, we praise thy Name All glory be to God on high Alleluia! sing to Jesus (st. 3) Hail, thou once despised Jesus	,, ,,	,, ,,
8:37	548	Soldiers of Christ, arise	,, ,,	,, ,,
8:38–39	693	Just as I am, without one plea	,, ,,	,, ,,
10:8–13	248, 249 252 435	To the Name of our salvation Jesus! Name of wondrous love At the Name of Jesus	5 Lent—Tuesday Proper 10—Sunday St. Matthew—Morning Prayer	Proper 9—Friday St. Matthew—Morning Prayer
11:33–36	677	God moves in a mysterious way	5 Lent—Saturday Proper 11—Sunday	Proper 10—Wednesday
12:1–21	610	Lord, whose love through humble service	5 Easter—Tuesday Proper 11—Sunday The Patronal Feast—Evening Prayer	5 Epiphany—Wednesday 5 Epiphany—Thursday 5 Lent—Sunday Proper 10—Thursday Proper 10—Friday The Patronal Feast—Evening Prayer
12:1	707	Take my life, and let it be	,, ,,	5 Epiphany—Wednesday 5 Lent—Sunday Proper 10—Thursday The Patronal Feast—Evening Prayer

Lectionary A	Lectionary B	Lectionary C	Pastoral Offices & Episcopal Services	Book of Occasional Services	Lesser Feasts and Fasts
Proper 13	See Above		Burial	Public Service of Healing Burial	Ignatius
,,　　,,	,,　　,,		,,　　,,	Public Service of Healing	
,,　　,,	,,　　,,		,,　　,,	Public Service of Healing Burial	Ignatius
,,　　,,	,,　　,,		,,　　,,	,,　　,,	
St. Andrew	St. Andrew	1 Lent St. Andrew			Dominic Charles Simeon
Proper 16 Of the Holy Trinity	Of the Holy Trinity	Of the Holy Trinity			
Proper 17 Proper 18 At Confirmation	At Confirmation	At Confirmation	New Ministry	Lay Ministries	John Keble Mary and Martha of Bethany
Proper 17 At Confirmation	,,　　,,	,,　　,,	,,　　,,		

			Daily Office Year One	Daily Office Year Two
12:4–8	513	Like the murmur of the dove's song	5 Easter—Tuesday The Patronal Feast—Evening Prayer	See Above
12:4–5	576, 577 581 606	God is love, and where true love is Where charity and love prevail Where true charity and love dwell	,, ,,	,, ,,
12:6–8	228 501, 502	Holy Spirit, font of life O Holy Spirit, by whose breath	,, ,,	,, ,,
12:9–21	593	Lord, make us servants of your peace	5 Easter—Tuesday Proper 12—Sunday The Patronal Feast—Evening Prayer	5 Epiphany—Thursday 5 Lent—Sunday Proper 10—Friday The Patronal Feast—Evening Prayer
12:17	347	Go forth for God; go to the world in peace	,, ,,	,, ,,
13:11–14	547	Awake, O sleeper, rise from death	5 Easter—Wednesday	5 Epiphany—Friday Proper 11—Monday
13:11–12	59 61, 62	Hark! a thrilling voice is sounding "Sleepers, wake!" A voice astounds us	,, ,,	,, ,,
14:9	478 494	Jesus, our mighty Lord Crown him with many crowns	5 Easter—Thursday Proper 13—Sunday	5 Epiphany—Saturday Proper 11—Tuesday
14:11	60 252	Creator of the stars of night Jesus! Name of wondrous love	,, ,,	,, ,,

Lectionary A	Lectionary B	Lectionary C	Pastoral Offices & Episcopal Services	Book of Occasional Services	Lesser Feasts and Fasts
See Above	See Above	See Above	See Above	See Above	
,, ,,	,, ,,	,, ,,	,, ,,	,, ,,	
,, ,,	,, ,,	,, ,,	,, ,,	,, ,,	
Proper 18			,, ,,	,, ,,	,, ,,
,, ,,			,, ,,		John Keble
1 Advent					
,, ,,					
Proper 19					Jeremy Taylor
,, ,,					,, ,,

				Daily Office Year One	Daily Office Year Two
15:4	628 630 631 632	Help us, O Lord, to learn Thanks to God whose Word was spoken Book of books, our people's strength O Christ, the Word Incarnate		5 Easter—Saturday Proper 14—Sunday	Proper 11—Thursday
15:7	603, 604	When Christ was lifted from the earth		Eve of Epiphany 5 Easter—Saturday Proper 14—Sunday Proper 29—Sunday	Eve of Epiphany Proper 11—Thursday Proper 29—Friday
15:13	344 472	Lord, dismiss us with thy blessing Hope of the world, thou Christ of great compassion		,,　　　,,	,,　　　,,

1 Corinthians:

				Daily Office Year One	Daily Office Year Two
1:10	576, 577 581 606	God is love, and where true love is Where charity and love prevail Where true charity and love dwell		Proper 19—Monday	1 Lent—Monday
1:18–25	165, 166	Sing, my tongue, the glorious battle		1 Lent—Sunday Proper 19—Monday Proper 19—Tuesday	1 Lent—Monday 1 Lent—Tuesday
1:18–24	434 471	Nature with open volume stands We sing the praise of him who died		,,　　　,,	,,　　　,,
2:9	61, 62	"Sleepers, wake!" A voice astounds us		The Day of Pentecost Proper 19—Wednesday	1 Lent—Wednesday Proper 22—Sunday

Lectionary A	Lectionary B	Lectionary C	Pastoral Offices & Episcopal Services	Book of Occasional Services	Lesser Feasts and Fasts
2 Advent					
,, ,,					
,, ,,					
3 Epiphany					
4 Epiphany Tuesday in Holy Week Of the Holy Cross	Tuesday in Holy Week Of the Holy Cross	Tuesday in Holy Week Of the Holy Cross		Special Vocation	Justin
,, ,,	,, ,,	,, ,,		,, ,,	,, ,,

5 Epiphany
Of a Theologian and
    Teacher I
	Of a Theologian and
	    Teacher I
		Of a Theologian and
		    Teacher I
					Basil the Great
					Richard Hooker

			Daily Office Year One	Daily Office Year Two
3:11–15	**636, 637**	How firm a foundation, ye saints of the Lord	2 Lent—Sunday Proper 19—Thursday Eve of the Dedication	1 Lent—Thursday Proper 29—Tuesday Eve of the Dedication
3:11	**518** **525**	Christ is made the sure foundation The Church's one foundation	,, ,,	,, ,,
3:16	**500** **516** **656**	Creator Spirit, by whose aid Come down, O Love divine Blest are the pure in heart	2 Lent—Sunday Proper 19—Friday Eve of the Dedication	1 Lent—Friday Proper 29—Tuesday Eve of the Dedication
5:7–8	**174** **183** **184** **185, 186** **202**	At the Lamb's high feast we sing Christians, to the Paschal victim Christ the Lord is risen again Christ Jesus lay in death's strong bands The Lamb's high banquet called to share	Proper 20—Tuesday	2 Lent—Tuesday
5:7	**307**	Lord, enthroned in heavenly splendor	,, ,,	,, ,,
6:11	**295**	Sing praise to our Creator		
6:19–20	**656**	Blest are the pure in heart	3 Lent—Sunday Proper 20—Thursday	2 Lent—Thursday
6:19	**500** **516**	Creator Spirit, by whose aid Come down, O Love divine	,, ,,	,, ,,
9:24–27	**422**	Not far beyond the sea, nor high (st. 3)	5 Lent—Sunday Proper 21—Friday	3 Lent—Friday

Lectionary A	Lectionary B	Lectionary C	Pastoral Offices & Episcopal Services	Book of Occasional Services	Lesser Feasts and Fasts
7 Epiphany Proper II Of a Theologian and Teacher II For the Ministry I For Rogation Days II For Labor Day	Of a Theologian and Teacher II For the Ministry I For Rogation Days II For Labor Day	Of a Theologian and Teacher II For the Ministry I For Rogation Days II For Labor Day	Consecration of a Church		James Lloyd Breck Jackson Kemper Columba Latimer, Ridley, and Cranmer
,, ,,	,, ,,	,, ,,	,, ,,		,, ,,
7 Epiphany Proper 2			,, ,,		Columba
Easter Day—Evening Service	Easter Day—Evening Service	Easter Day—Evening Service			
,, ,,	,, ,,	,, ,,			
	2 Epiphany				
	,, ,,				
	,, ,,				
	6 Epiphany Proper 1				

			Daily Office Year One	Daily Office Year Two
9:24–26	552, 553	Fight the good fight with all thy might	See Above	See Above
9:24–25	546	Awake, my soul, stretch every nerve	,, ,,	,, ,,
9:24	27, 28	O blest Creator, source of light	,, ,,	,, ,,
10:1–4	149 187 343 522, 523 690	Eternal Lord of love, behold your Church Through the Red Sea brought at last Shepherd of souls, refresh and bless Glorious things of thee are spoken Guide me, O thou great Jehovah	Proper 21—Saturday	3 Lent—Saturday Proper 24—Sunday
10:3–4	307 308, 309 332 685	Lord, enthroned in heavenly splendor O Food to pilgrims given O God, unseen yet ever near Rock of ages, cleft for me	,, ,,	,, ,,
10:12–13	142 143 146, 147 150	Lord, who throughout these forty days The glory of these forty days Now let us all with one accord Forty days and forty nights	,, ,,	,, ,,
10:16–17	304 305, 306 315	I come with joy to meet my Lord Come, risen Lord, and deign to be our guest Thou, who at thy first Eucharist didst pray	Maundy Thursday Proper22—Monday	4 Lent—Monday Maundy Thursday Proper 25—Sunday
10:16	327, 328	Draw nigh and take the Body of the Lord	,, ,,	,, ,,
10:17	525	The Church's one foundation (st. 2)	,, ,,	,, ,,
10:31	626	Lord, be thy word my rule	Proper 22—Monday	4 Lent—Monday

Lectionary A	Lectionary B	Lectionary C	Pastoral Offices & Episcopal Services	Book of Occasional Services	Lesser Feasts and Fasts
	See Above				
	,, ,,				
	,, ,,				
Of the Holy Eucharist	Of the Holy Eucharist	3 Lent Of the Holy Eucharist			
,, ,,	,, ,,	,, ,,			
		3 Lent			
,, ,,	,, ,,	Of the Holy Eucharist			
,, ,,	,, ,,	,, ,,			
,, ,,	,, ,,	,, ,,			

			Daily Office Year One	Daily Office Year Two
11:23–26	**51**	We the Lord's people, heart and voice uniting	Proper 22—Wednesday	4 Lent—Tuesday
	174	At the Lamb's high feast we sing		
	305, 306	Come, risen Lord, and deign to be our guest		
	320	Zion, praise thy Savior, singing		
	322	When Jesus died to save us		
	329, 330, 331	Now, my tongue, the mystery telling		
	340, 341	For the bread which you have broken		
	528	Lord, you give the great commission (st. 3)		
11:24	**342**	O Bread of life, for sinners broken	,,　　,,	,,　　,,
11:27–32	**339**	Deck thyself, my soul, with gladness	Maundy Thursday Proper 22—Wednesday	4 Lent—Tuesday Maundy Thursday
12:3	**505**	O Spirit of Life, O Spirit of God	Proper 22—Thursday	4 Lent—Wednesday
	506, 507	Praise the Spirit in creation		
12:4–11	**228**	Holy Spirit, font of light	,,　　,,	,,　　,,
	501, 502	O Holy Spirit, by whose breath		
12:12–31	**295**	Sing praise to our Creator	Proper 22—Friday	4 Lent—Thursday
	296	We know that Christ is raised and dies no more	Proper 22—Saturday	4 Lent—Friday
12:12–27	**513**	Like the murmur of the dove's song	,,　　,,	,,　　,,
12:12–13, 27	**576, 577**	God is love, and where true love is	,,　　,,	,,　　,,
	581	Where charity and love prevail		Proper 26—Sunday
	606	Where true charity and love dwell		

Lectionary A	Lectionary B	Lectionary C	Pastoral Offices & Episcopal Services	Book of Occasional Services	Lesser Feasts and Fasts
Maundy Thursday Of the Holy Eucharist	Maundy Thursday Of the Holy Eucharist	Maundy Thursday Of the Holy Eucharist			
,, ,,	,, ,,	,, ,,			
,, ,,	,, ,,	,, ,,			
		2 Epiphany			
Day of Pentecost— Principal Service Of the Holy Spirit	Day of Pentecost— Principal Service Of the Holy Spirit	2 Epiphany Day of Pentecost— Principal Service Of the Holy Spirit			
,, ,,	,, ,,	3 Epiphany Last Epiphany Day of Pentecost— Principal Service Of the Holy Spirit			
,, ,,	,, ,,	,, ,,			
,, ,,	,, ,,	,, ,,			

			Daily Office Year One	Daily Office Year Two
13:1–13	612	Gracious Spirit, Holy Ghost	Proper 22—Saturday Proper 23—Monday	4 Lent—Friday Proper 26—Sunday
15:3–4, 20–23, 35–56	204	Now the green blade riseth	Proper 23—Friday Proper 23—Saturday Proper 24—Monday Proper 24—Tuesday Proper 25—Wednesday	Easter Week—Monday Easter Week—Tuesday Easter Week—Wednesday Easter Week—Thursday Easter Week—Friday
15:3–8	452	Glorious the day when Christ was born	Proper 23—Friday	Easter Week—Monday
15:7	231, 232	By all your saints still striving (Saint James of Jerusalem)	,, ,,	,, ,,
15:10	671 686	Amazing grace! how sweet the sound Come, thou fount of every blessing	,, ,,	,, ,,
15:16–20	192	This joyful Eastertide	Proper 23—Saturday	Easter Week—Tuesday
15:20–23, 35–50	191	Alleluia, alleluia! Hearts and voices heavenward raise	Proper 23—Saturday Proper 24—Monday Proper 24—Tuesday	Easter Week—Tuesday Easter Week—Wednesday Easter Week—Thursday
15:21–22	445, 446	Praise to the Holiest in the height	Proper 23—Saturday	Easter Week—Tuesday

Lectionary A	Lectionary B	Lectionary C	Pastoral Offices & Episcopal Services	Book of Occasional Services	Lesser Feasts and Fasts
		Last Epiphany	Marriage		
Proper 29 St. James of Jerusalem For the Departed	St. James of Jerusalem For the Departed	5 Epiphany 6 Epiphany 7 Epiphany 8 Epiphany Proper 1 Proper 2 Proper 3 St. James of Jerusalem For the Departed	Burial		John of Damascus All Faithful Departed
St. James of Jerusalem	St. James of Jerusalem	5 Epiphany St. James of Jerusalem			
,, ,,	,, ,,	,, ,,			
,, ,,	,, ,,	,, ,,			
Proper 29		6 Epiphany Proper 1	Burial		John of Damascus
,, ,, For the Departed		,, ,, 7 Epiphany 8 Epiphany Proper 2 Proper 3 For the Departed	,, ,,		John of Damascus All Faithful Departed
Proper 29			,, ,,		

			Daily Office Year One	Daily Office Year Two
15:24–28	**492**	Sing, ye faithful, sing with gladness	See Above	See Above
15:30–58	**621, 622**	Light's abode, celestial Salem	Proper 24—Monday Proper 24—Tuesday Proper 24—Wednesday	Easter Week—Wednesday Easter Week—Thursday Easter Week—Friday
15:51–57	**192**	This joyful Eastertide	Proper 24—Wednesday	Easter Week—Friday
15:54–57	**188, 189** **208** **220, 221** **358**	Love's redeeming work is done The strife is o'er, the battle done O Lord Most High, eternal King Christ the Victorious, give to your servants	,, ,,	,, ,,
15:55–57	**364** **366** **472**	O God, we praise thee, and confess Holy God, we praise thy Name Hope of the world, thou Christ of great compassion	,, ,,	,, ,,
15:55	**662**	Abide with me: fast falls the eventide	,, ,,	,, ,,
16:1–4	**9** **705**	Not here for high and holy things As those of old their first fruits brought	Proper 24—Thursday	

Lectionary A	Lectionary B	Lectionary C	Pastoral Offices & Episcopal Services	Book of Occasional Services	Lesser Feasts and Fasts
See Above		See Above	See Above		
For the Departed	For the Departed	7 Epiphany Proper 2 Proper 3 For the Departed	Burial		All Faithful Departed
,, ,,	,, ,,	8 Epiphany Proper 3 For the Departed	,, ,,		,, ,,
,, ,,	,, ,,	,, ,,	,, ,,		,, ,,
,, ,,	,, ,,	,, ,,	,, ,,		,, ,,
,, ,,	,, ,,	,, ,,	,, ,,		,, ,,

2 Corinthians:

			Daily Office Year One	Daily Office Year Two
1:20–22	697	My God, accept my heart this day	7 Epiphany—Tuesday Proper 3—Tuesday	Holy Week—Tuesday
1:21–22	686	Come, thou fount of every blessing	,, ,,	,, ,,
3:6	505	O Spirit of Life, O Spirit of God	7 Epiphany—Thursday Proper 3—Thursday Eve of the Transfiguration	5 Lent—Wednesday Eve of the Transfiguration
3:18	133, 134 136, 137 326 620 657	O Light of Light, Love given birth (st. 3) O wondrous type! O vision fair (st. 5) From glory to glory advancing, we praise thee, O Lord Jerusalem, my happy home Love divine, all loves excelling	,, ,,	Last Epiphany—Sunday 5 Lent—Thursday Eve of the Transfiguration
4:6	5 6, 7 381 419 465, 466	O splendor of God's glory bright Christ, whose glory fills the skies Thy strong word did cleave the darkness Lord of all being, throned afar Eternal light, shine in my heart	7 Epiphany—Friday Proper 3—Friday The Transfiguration—Morning Prayer	5 Lent—Friday The Transfiguration—Morning Prayer
4:14	194, 195	Jesus lives! thy terrors now	7 Epiphany—Saturday	5 Lent—Saturday
4:16—5:10	621, 622 623	Light's abode, celestial Salem O what their joy and their glory must be	,, ,,	Easter Week—Saturday
5:7	209	We walk by faith, and not by sight	,, ,,	,, ,,
5:8	620	Jerusalem, my happy home	,, ,,	,, ,,

Lectionary A	Lectionary B	Lectionary C	Pastoral Offices & Episcopal Services	Book of Occasional Services	Lesser Feasts and Fasts
	7 Epiphany Proper 2				
	,, ,,				
	8 Epiphany Proper 3		Ordination: Bishop		
	,, ,,				
SS. Philip & James For a Church Convention	Proper 4 SS. Philip & James For a Church Convention	SS. Philip & James For a Church Convention	Ordination: Deacon	Lay Ministries	
	Proper 5				Samuel Isaac Joseph Schereschewsky
	Proper 5 Proper 6		Burial		,, ,,
	Proper 6		,, ,,		
	,, ,,		,, ,,		

			Daily Office Year One	Daily Office Year Two
5:10	63, 64	O heavenly Word, eternal Light	See Above	See Above
5:17	176, 177 213 296 298	Over the chaos of the empty waters Come away to the skies We know that Christ is raised and dies no more All who believe and are baptized	December 31 Proper 4—Monday	7 Epiphany—Sunday
5:18–19	603, 604	When Christ was lifted from the earth	,, ,,	,, ,,
5:21	492	Sing, ye faithful, sing with gladness	,, ,,	,, ,,
6:3–10	559	Lead us, heavenly Father, lead us	Proper 4—Tuesday	
6:16–18	500 656	Creator Spirit, by whose aid Blest are the pure in heart	,, ,,	
7:9–11	144 148 152 574, 575	Lord Jesus, Sun of Righteousness Creator of the earth and skies Kind Maker of the world, O hear Before thy throne, O God, we kneel	Proper 4—Wednesday	
8:1–15	9 705	Not here for high and holy things As those of old their first fruits brought	Proper 4—Thursday	
8:5	707	Take my life, and let it be	,, ,,	
8:8–15	292	O Jesus, crowned with all renown	,, ,,	

Lectionary A	Lectionary B	Lectionary C	Pastoral Offices & Episcopal Services	Book of Occasional Services	Lesser Feasts and Fasts
	See Above				
St. Mary Magdalene At Baptism	Proper 7 St. Mary Magdalene At Baptism	4 Lent St. Mary Magdalene At Baptism		New Year's Eve Vigil Before Baptism	Augustine of Canterbury
,,　　,,	,,　　,,	,,　　,,		,,　　,,	,,　　,,
Ash Wednesday	Proper 7 Ash Wednesday	4 Lent Ash Wednesday		New Year's Eve	
,,　　,, Of a Monastic II	,,　　,, Of a Monastic II	,,　　,, Of a Monastic II			Cuthbert
	Proper 8				
	,,　　,,				
	,,　　,,				Laurence

			Daily Office Year One	Daily Office Year Two
9:1–15	**9**	Not here for high and holy things	Proper 4—Saturday	8 Epiphany—Sunday
	705	As those of old their first fruits brought		Proper 13—Sunday
12:9	**548**	Soldiers of Christ, arise	8 Epiphany—Thursday	
	636, 637	How firm a foundation, ye saints of the Lord	Proper 5—Thursday	
13:14	**351**	May the grace of Christ our Savior	8 Epiphany—Saturday	
			Proper 5—Saturday	

Galatians:

			Daily Office Year One	Daily Office Year Two
1:11–24	**231, 232**	By all your saints still striving (Conversion of Saint Paul)	3 Epiphany—Monday	Proper 4—Monday
			3 Epiphany—Tuesday	Proper 4—Tuesday
	255	We sing the glorious conquest		
	256	A light from heaven shone around		
1:18–19	**231, 232**	By all your saints still striving (Saint James of Jerusalem)	3 Epiphany—Tuesday	Proper 4—Tuesday
2:1–10	**231, 232**	By all your saints still striving (Saint James of Jerusalem)	3 Epiphany—Tuesday	3 Epiphany—Sunday
			SS. Peter & Paul—Evening Prayer	Proper 4—Tuesday
				SS. Peter & Paul—Evening Prayer
2:20	**697**	My God, accept my heart this day	3 Epiphany—Wednesday	Proper 4—Wednesday
3:10–14	**270**	Gabriel's message does away	3 Epiphany—Thursday	4 Advent—Thursday
			Proper 15—Sunday	Proper 4—Thursday

Lectionary A	Lectionary B	Lectionary C	Pastoral Offices & Episcopal Services	Book of Occasional Services	Lesser Feasts and Fasts
					Laurence
	Proper 9				
Trinity Sunday					
Conversion of St. Paul	Conversion of St. Paul	Proper 5 Conversion of St. Paul			
,,　　,,	,,　　,,	,,　　,,			
		Proper 6			The Martyrs of Japan

			Daily Office Year One	Daily Office Year Two
3:23—4:7	294 295	Baptized in water Sing praise to our Creator	Eve of 1 Epiphany 3 Epiphany—Saturday 4 Epiphany—Monday Proper 16—Sunday	December 24 Eve of 1 Epiphany Proper 4—Saturday
3:27–28	529	In Christ there is no East or West	Eve of 1 Epiphany 3 Epiphany—Saturday Proper 16—Sunday	” ”
3:28	581	Where charity and love prevail	” ”	” ”
5:22	513	Like the murmur of the dove's song	4 Epiphany—Friday	4 Epiphany—Sunday Proper 5—Thursday
5:24	697	My God, accept my heart this day	” ”	” ”
6:14	165, 166 178 434 441, 442 471 474 483 498 697	Sing, my tongue, the glorious battle Jesus is Lord of all the earth (st. 3) Nature with open volume stands In the cross of Christ I glory We sing the praise of him who died When I survey the wondrous cross The head that once was crowned with thorns Beneath the cross of Jesus My God, accept my heart this day	5 Epiphany—Monday	Proper 5—Saturday
6:15	176, 177 296	Over the chaos of the empty waters We know that Christ is raised and dies no more	” ”	” ”

Lectionary A	Lectionary B	Lectionary C	Pastoral Offices & Episcopal Services	Book of Occasional Services	Lesser Feasts and Fasts
1 Christmas	1 Christmas	1 Christmas Proper 7			William Wilberforce
		Proper 7			,, ,,
		,, ,,			,, ,,
At Confirmation	At Confirmation	Proper 8 At Confirmation			
,, ,,	,, ,,	,, ,,			
Holy Cross Day	Holy Cross Day	Proper 9 Holy Cross Day			Francis of Assisi James Otis Sargent Huntington
,, ,,	,, ,,	,, ,,			,, ,,

Ephesians:

			Daily Office Year One	Daily Office Year Two
1:3–4	706	In your mercy, Lord, you called me	1 Epiphany—Monday	1 Epiphany—Sunday 6 Easter—Wednesday Proper 29—Wednesday
1:4–6	295	Sing praise to our Creator	,, ,,	,, ,,
1:5–8	671 686	Amazing grace! how sweet the sound Come, thou fount of every blessing	,, ,,	,, ,,
1:7–8	469, 470	There's a wideness in God's mercy	,, ,,	,, ,,
1:7	38, 39 434 495	Jesus, Redeemer of the world Nature with open volume stands Hail, thou once despised Jesus	,, ,,	,, ,,
1:10	492	Sing, ye faithful, sing with gladness	,, ,,	,, ,,
1:13–14	294 514 686 697	Baptized in water To thee, O Comforter divine Come, thou fount of every blessing My God, accept my heart this day	,, ,,	1 Epiphany—Sunday Proper 29—Wednesday
1:20	364 366 421	O God, we praise thee, and confess Holy God, we praise thy Name All glory be to God on high	1 Epiphany—Tuesday	
1:22–23	518	Christ is made the sure foundation	,, ,,	
2:4–10	671 706	Amazing grace! how sweet the sound In your mercy, Lord, you called me	1 Epiphany—Wednesday 7 Easter—Sunday	6 Easter—Friday

Lectionary A	Lectionary B	Lectionary C	Pastoral Offices & Episcopal Services	Book of Occasional Services	Lesser Feasts and Fasts
2 Christmas	2 Christmas Proper 10	2 Christmas			William Reed Huntington
,, ,,	,, ,,	,, ,,			,, ,,
,, ,,	,, ,,	,, ,,			,, ,,
	Proper 10				,, ,,
	,, ,,				,, ,,
	,, ,,				,, ,,
All Saints' Day	Proper 10 All Saints' Day	All Saints' Day			
Ascension Day All Saints' Day	Ascension Day All Saints' Day	Ascension Day All Saints' Day			
,, ,,	,, ,,	,, ,,			
	4 Lent				

			Daily Office Year One	Daily Office Year Two
2:8–10	686	Come, thou fount of every blessing	See Above	See Above
2:8–9	151	From deepest woe I cry to thee	,, ,,	,, ,,
2:8	685	Rock of ages, cleft for me	,, ,,	,, ,,
2:13–16	693	Just as I am, without one plea	1 Epiphany—Thursday Eve of Holy Cross	6 Easter—Saturday Eve of Holy Cross
2:14–16	495	Hail, thou once despised Jesus	,, ,,	,, ,,
2:19–22	235 518 525	Come sing, ye choirs exultant (st. 3) Christ is made the sure foundation The Church's one foundation	,, ,,	,, ,,
3:14–19	422 693	Not far beyond the sea, nor high (st. 2) Just as I am, without one plea	1 Epiphany—Saturday Eve of Trinity Sunday St. Joseph—Evening Prayer	7 Easter—Tuesday Eve of Trinity Sunday St. Joseph—Evening Prayer
3:17–19	448, 449 455, 456	O love, how deep, how broad, how high O Love of God, how strong and true	,, ,,	,, ,,
3:18–19	547	Awake, O sleeper, rise from death (st. 1)	,, ,,	,, ,,

Lectionary A	Lectionary B	Lectionary C	Pastoral Offices & Episcopal Services	Book of Occasional Services	Lesser Feasts and Fasts
	See Above				
	,, ,,				
	,, ,,				

SS. Simon & Jude
For the Mission of the
  Church I
For Peace
	Proper 11
	SS. Simon & Jude
	For the Mission of the
	  Church I
	For Peace
		SS. Simon & Jude
		For the Mission of the
		  Church I
		For Peace
					George Augustus Selwyn

,, ,,	,, ,,	,, ,,			,, ,,

SS. Simon & Jude
For the Mission of the
  Church I
	Proper 11
	SS. Simon & Jude
	For the Mission of the
	  Church I
		SS. Simon & Jude
		For the Mission of the
		  Church I			

Of a Pastor II	Of a Pastor II	Of a Pastor II	Marriage		Phillips Brooks Frederick Denison Maurice
,, ,,	,, ,,	,, ,,	,, ,,		,, ,,
,, ,,	,, ,,	,, ,,	,, ,,		,, ,,

			Daily Office Year One	Daily Office Year Two
4:1–16	521	Put forth, O God, thy Spirit's might	2 Epiphany—Monday Trinity Sunday SS. Simon & Jude—Morning Prayer Eve of the Patronal Feast	January 2 2 Epiphany—Sunday 7 Easter—Wednesday SS. Simon & Jude—Morning Prayer Eve of the Patronal Feast
4:3–5	547	Awake, O sleeper, rise from death (sts. 2–3)	,, ,,	,, ,,
4:4–6	305, 306	Come, risen Lord, and deign to be our guest	,, ,,	,, ,,
	525	The Church's one foundation (st. 2)		
	527	Singing songs of expectation		
	562	Onward, Christian soldiers		
	617	Eternal Ruler of the ceaseless round		
4:8–10	220, 221	O Lord Most High, eternal King	,, ,,	,, ,,
	492	Sing, ye faithful, sing with gladness		
4:25	576, 577	God is love, and where true love is	2 Epiphany—Tuesday	January 3 7 Easter—Thursday
	581	Where charity and love prevail		
	606	Where true charity and love dwell		
4:30	294	Baptized in water	,, ,,	,, ,,
	514	To thee, O Comforter divine		
4:31–32	576, 577	God is love, and where true love is	,, ,,	,, ,,
	581	Where charity and love prevail		
	606	Where true charity and love dwell		
4:32	547	Awake, O sleeper, rise from death (st. 4)	,, ,,	,, ,,

Lectionary A	Lectionary B	Lectionary C	Pastoral Offices & Episcopal Services	Book of Occasional Services	Lesser Feasts and Fasts
St. Mark At Confirmation For the Unity of the Church For the Ministry II	Proper 12 St. Mark At Confirmation For the Unity of the Church For the Ministry II	St. Mark At Confirmation For the Unity of the Church For the Ministry II	Ordination: Priest New Ministry		Charles Henry Brent William Augustus Muhlenberg William Reed Huntington Hilda
For the Unity of the Church	Proper 12 For the Unity of the Church	For the Unity of the Church			Charles Henry Brent Hilda
,, ,,	,, ,,	,, ,,			,, ,,
St. Mark	St. Mark	St. Mark			
	Proper 13				
	Proper 14				
	,, ,,				
	,, ,,				

			Daily Office Year One	Daily Office Year Two
5:2, 14	547	Awake, O sleeper, rise from death (st. 4)	2 Epiphany—Wednesday	January 4 7 Easter—Friday
5:8–14	490	I want to walk as a child of the light	,, ,,	,, ,,
5:19	420 426	When in our music God is glorified Songs of praise the angels sang	2 Epiphany—Thursday	,, ,,
5:23–32	519, 520 524 525	Blessed city, heavenly Salem I love thy kingdom, Lord The Church's one foundation	,, ,,	
5:30	576, 577 581 606	God is love, and where true love is Where charity and love prevail Where true charity and love dwell	,, ,,	
5:31	350 352	O God of love, to thee we bow O God, to those who here profess	,, ,,	
6:10–17	548 561 617	Soldiers of Christ, arise Stand up, stand up for Jesus Eternal Ruler of the ceaseless round	4 Advent—Sunday 2 Epiphany—Saturday	January 5 7 Easter—Saturday

Philippians:

1:9–11	344 392	Lord, dismiss us with thy blessing Come, we that love the Lord	Proper 18—Monday	8 Epiphany—Saturday

Lectionary A	Lectionary B	Lectionary C	Pastoral Offices & Episcopal Services	Book of Occasional Services	Lesser Feasts and Fasts
4 Lent	See Above		Marriage		
,, ,,	Proper 15				
	Proper 16				
	,, ,,		Marriage		
	,, ,,		,, ,,		
	,, ,,		,, ,,		
	Proper 17				
		2 Advent			

			Daily Office Year One	Daily Office Year Two
2:5–11	60	Creator of the stars of night	Christmas Eve	Christmas Eve
	160	Cross of Jesus, cross of sorrow	Proper 18—Wednesday	Last Epiphany—Monday
	248, 249	To the Name of our salvation		Proper 29—Saturday
	252	Jesus! Name of wondrous love		
	307	Lord, enthroned in heavenly splendor		
	435	At the Name of Jesus		
	450, 451	All hail the power of Jesus' Name		
	477	All praise to thee, for thou, O King divine		
	483	The head that once was crowned with thorns		
	492	Sing, ye faithful, sing with gladness		
	585	Morning glory, starlit sky (st. 4)		
2:6–11	439	What wondrous love is this	,, ,,	,, ,,
2:9–11	427	When morning gilds the skies	,, ,,	,, ,,
2:10–11	531	O Spirit of the living God (st. 4)	,, ,,	,, ,,
2:16	546	Awake, my soul, stretch every nerve	Proper 18—Thursday	
3:7–11	471	We sing the praise of him who died	Holy Week—Monday	Last Epiphany—Tuesday
	474	When I survey the wondrous cross	Proper 18—Friday	Conversion of St. Paul—Morning Prayer
	701	Jesus, all my gladness	Conversion of St. Paul—Morning Prayer	
3:12–14	545	Lo! what a cloud of witnesses	Holy Week—Monday	Last Epiphany—Thursday
	546	Awake, my soul, stretch every nerve	Proper 18—Friday	Proper 28—Sunday
3:14	27, 28	O blest Creator, source of light	,, ,,	,, ,,
	422	Not far beyond the sea, nor high (st. 3)		

Lectionary A	Lectionary B	Lectionary C	Pastoral Offices & Episcopal Services	Book of Occasional Services	Lesser Feasts and Fasts
Holy Name Palm Sunday Proper 21 Holy Cross Day Oppression (GC 82)	Palm Sunday Holy Cross Day Oppression (GC 82)	Palm Sunday Holy Cross Day Oppression (GC 82)			
,, ,,	,, ,,	,, ,,			
,, ,,	,, ,,	,, ,,			
,, ,,	,, ,,	,, ,,			
Last Epiphany Of a Monastic I	Of a Monastic I	5 Lent Of a Monastic I		Special Vocation	William Law
Last Epiphany Proper 22 St. Matthias Of a Monastic I	St. Matthias Of a Monastic I	5 Lent St. Matthias Of a Monastic I		,, ,,	,, ,,
,, ,,	,, ,,	,, ,,		,, ,,	,, ,,

			Daily Office Year One	Daily Office Year Two
3:20–21	**621, 622**	Light's abode, celestial Salem	Holy Week—Tuesday Proper 18—Saturday	See Above
4:4	**481**	Rejoice, the Lord is King	Holy Week—Wednesday Proper 18—Saturday	Last Epiphany—Friday
4:7	**345**	Saviour, again to thy dear Name we raise	,, ,,	,, ,,

Colossians:

			Daily Office Year One	Daily Office Year Two
1:9–10	**344** **392**	Lord, dismiss us with thy blessing Come, we that love the Lord	4 Easter—Monday	1 Christmas January 7 3 Easter—Tuesday 6 Easter—Monday
1:11–20	**467**	Sing, my soul, his wondrous love	4 Easter—Monday 4 Easter—Tuesday	1 Christmas January 7 3 Easter—Tuesday 3 Easter—Wednesday 6 Easter—Monday
1:11–12	**326**	From glory to glory advancing, we praise thee, O Lord	4 Easter—Monday	1 Christmas January 7 3 Easter—Tuesday 6 Easter—Monday
1:15–20	**82** **421**	Of the Father's love begotten All glory be to God on high	4 Easter—Tuesday	1 Christmas January 8 3 Easter—Wednesday

Lectionary A	Lectionary B	Lectionary C	Pastoral Offices & Episcopal Services	Book of Occasional Services	Lesser Feasts and Fasts
Proper 22 St. Matthias	St. Matthias	St. Matthias			
Proper 23 Of a Saint II	Of a Saint II	4 Advent Of a Saint II	Ordination: Priest		Thomas Ken Thomas a Kempis
,, ,,	,, ,,	,, ,,	,, ,,		,, ,,
		Proper 10			
Of the Reign of Christ	Of the Reign of Christ	Proper 10 Proper 29 Of the Reign of Christ		Public Service of Healing	Clement of Alexandria
,, ,,	,, ,,	,, ,,		,, ,,	,, ,,
,, ,,	,, ,,	Proper 29 Of the Reign of Christ		,, ,,	,, ,,

			Daily Office Year One	Daily Office Year Two
1:18	**307**	Lord, enthroned in heavenly splendor	See Above	See Above
	518	Christ is made the sure foundation		
1:19–23	**495**	Hail, thou once despised Jesus	,, ,,	,, ,,
2:12–14	**47**	On this day, the first of days	Holy Name	January 10
	294	Baptized in water	4 Easter—Thursday	3 Easter—Friday
	298	All who believe and are baptized		
3:1	**364**	O God, we praise thee, and confess	4 Easter—Friday	January 11
	366	Holy God, we praise thy Name		3 Easter—Saturday
3:11	**529**	In Christ there is no East or West	,, ,,	,, ,,
	542	Christ is the world's true Light		
	581	Where charity and love prevail		
3:12–15	**576, 577**	God is love, and where true love is	4 Easter—Saturday	2 Christmas
	581	Where charity and love prevail		January 11
	593	Lord, make us servants of your peace		3 Easter—Saturday
	606	Where true charity and love dwell		
3:13	**674**	Forgive our sins as we forgive	,, ,,	,, ,,
3:16	**420**	When in our music God is glorified	,, ,,	,, ,,
	426	Songs of praise the angels sang		
3:17	**592**	Teach me, my God and King	,, ,,	,, ,,
	661	Christ the worker		
4:14	**231, 232**	By all your saints still striving (Saint Luke)	5 Easter—Monday	4 Easter—Monday

Lectionary A	Lectionary B	Lectionary C	Pastoral Offices & Episcopal Services	Book of Occasional Services	Lesser Feasts and Fasts
See Above	See Above	See Above		See Above	See Above
,, ,,	,, ,,	Proper 11 Proper 29 Of the Reign of Christ		,, ,,	,, ,,
		Proper 12			
Easter Day—Principal Service	Easter Day—Principal Service	Easter Day—Principal Service			
		Proper 13			
The Visitation For Peace	The Visitation For Peace	Proper 13 The Visitation For Peace	Marriage	Lay Ministries Special Vocation	
,, ,,	,, ,,	,, ,,	,, ,,	,, ,,	
The Visitation	The Visitation	Proper 13 The Visitation	,, ,,	,, ,,	
,, ,,	,, ,,	,, ,,	,, ,,	,, ,,	

1 Thessalonians:

			Daily Office Year One	Daily Office Year Two
2:19–20	383, 384	Fairest Lord Jesus	1 Advent—Wednesday	4 Easter—Thursday
3:11–13	63, 64	O heavenly Word, eternal Light	1 Advent—Thursday	4 Easter—Friday
4:13–17	192 194, 195	This joyful Eastertide Jesus lives! thy terrors now	1 Advent—Saturday	5 Easter—Monday
4:16–17	57, 58	Lo! he comes, with clouds descending	,, ,,	,, ,,
5, 6	547	Awake, O sleeper, rise from death	2 Advent—Monday	1 Advent—Sunday 5 Easter—Tuesday
5:8	548 561 617	Soldiers of Christ, arise Stand up, stand up for Jesus Eternal Ruler of the ceaseless round	,, ,,	,, ,,
5:14–21	347	Go forth for God; go to the world in peace	2 Advent—Tuesday Thanksgiving Day—Evening Prayer	5 Easter—Wednesday Thanksgiving Day—Evening Prayer

2 Thessalonians:

1:7–10	57, 58	Lo! he comes, with clouds descending	2 Advent—Wednesday	2 Advent—Sunday 5 Easter—Thursday
2:13	295	Sing praise to our Creator	2 Advent—Friday 5 Easter—Sunday	3 Advent—Sunday 5 Easter—Friday

Lectionary A	Lectionary B	Lectionary C	Pastoral Offices & Episcopal Services	Book of Occasional Services	Lesser Feasts and Fasts
Proper 26					
Proper 27					All Faithful Departed
,, ,,					,, ,,
Proper 28					
,, ,,					
	2 Advent				
		Proper 26			
		Proper 27			

			Daily Office Year One	Daily Office Year Two
3:6–15	9 11	Not here for high and holy things Awake, my soul, and with the sun	2 Advent—Saturday	5 Easter—Saturday
3:16	345	Savior, again to thy dear Name we raise	,, ,,	,, ,,

1 Timothy:

			Daily Office Year One	Daily Office Year Two
1:1	472	Hope of the world, thou Christ of great compassion	6 Epiphany—Monday Proper 2—Monday	Proper 3—Monday
1:17	423	Immortal, invisible, God only wise	,, ,,	,, ,,
2:5–6	368	Holy Father, great Creator	6 Epiphany—Tuesday Proper 2—Tuesday	Proper 3—Tuesday
6:12	552, 553	Fight the good fight with all thy might	6 Epiphany—Saturday Palm Sunday Proper 2—Saturday	Palm Sunday Proper 3—Saturday
6:14–16	494	Crown him with many crowns	,, ,,	,, ,,
6:16	423	Immortal, invisible, God only wise	,, ,,	,, ,,

Lectionary A	Lectionary B	Lectionary C	Pastoral Offices & Episcopal Services	Book of Occasional Services	Lesser Feasts and Fasts
		Proper 28			
		Proper 20			
		Proper 21			
		,, ,,			
		,, ,,			

2 Timothy:

			Daily Office Year One	Daily Office Year Two
1:6–7	704	O thou who camest from above	5 Epiphany—Tuesday Proper 1—Monday	7 Epiphany—Saturday
1:8–10	151	From deepest woe I cry to thee	" "	" "
2:3–4	561	Stand up, stand up for Jesus	5 Epiphany—Wednesday Proper 1—Tuesday	8 Epiphany—Monday 6 Easter—Tuesday
2:3	548 562	Soldiers of Christ, arise Onward, Christian soldiers	" "	" "
2:11–12	483	The head that once was crowned with thorns	" "	8 Epiphany—Monday
2:21	707	Take my life, and let it be	5 Epiphany—Thursday Proper 1—Wednesday	5 Epiphany—Sunday 8 Epiphany—Tuesday
2:22	656	Blest are the pure in heart	" "	8 Epiphany—Tuesday
3:14–17	627 628 630 631	Lamp of our feet, whereby we trace Help us, O Lord, to learn Thanks to God whose Word was spoken Book of books, our people's strength	5 Epiphany—Friday Proper 1—Thursday	8 Epiphany—Wednesday
4:1	63, 64 364 366 421	O heavenly Word, eternal Light O God, we praise thee, and confess Holy God, we praise thy Name All glory be to God on high	5 Epiphany—Saturday 8 Epiphany—Sunday Proper 1—Friday St. Mark—Evening Prayer	8 Epiphany—Thursday St. Mark—Evening Prayer

Lectionary A	Lectionary B	Lectionary C	Pastoral Offices & Episcopal Services	Book of Occasional Services	Lesser Feasts and Fasts
		Proper 22			Timothy and Titus Leo the Great
		,, ,,			,, ,,
		Proper 23			Theodore of Tarsus Lancelot Andrewes Clement of Rome
		,, ,,			,, ,,
		,, ,,			James DeKoven
					Irenaeus
St. Matthew Of the Incarnation For Education	St. Matthew Of the Incarnation For Education	Proper 24 St. Matthew Of the Incarnation For Education			Jerome
SS. Peter & Paul For Education	SS. Peter & Paul For Education	Proper 24 SS. Peter & Paul For Education			

			Daily Office Year One	Daily Office Year Two
4:7–8	231, 232	By all your saints still striving	See Above	See Above
	286	Who are these like stars appearing		
	287	For all the saints, who from their labors rest		
	552, 553	Fight the good fight with all thy might		
	555	Lead on, O King eternal		
	561	Stand up, stand up for Jesus		
4:11	231, 232	By all your saints still striving (Saint Mark)	Proper 1—Saturday	8 Epiphany—Friday
	285	What thanks and praise to thee we owe	St. Mark—Evening Prayer	St. Mark—Evening Prayer
4:18	636, 637	How firm a foundation, ye saints of the Lord	,, ,,	,, ,,

Titus:

			Daily Office Year One	Daily Office Year Two
3:4–7	151	From deepest woe I cry to thee	Last Epiphany—Saturday	4 Advent—Wednesday
	294	Baptized in water		
	295	Sing praise to our Creator		
	296	We know that Christ is raised and dies no more		

Hebrews:

			Daily Office Year One	Daily Office Year Two
1:1–10; 25	495	Hail, thou once despised Jesus	See below	See below

Lectionary A	Lectionary B	Lectionary C	Pastoral Offices & Episcopal Services	Book of Occasional Services	Lesser Feasts and Fasts
SS. Peter & Paul For Education St. Luke	SS. Peter & Paul For Education St. Luke	Proper 25 SS. Peter & Paul For Education St. Luke			
St. Luke	St. Luke	St. Luke			
		Proper 25			
Christmas Day II	Christmas Day II	Christmas Day II			
See below	See below	See below		See below	

			Daily Office Year One	Daily Office Year Two
1:1—2:18	489	The great Creator of the worlds	See below	See below
1:1–14	448, 449 491	O love, how deep, how broad, how high Where is this stupendous stranger	1 Epiphany—Sunday Last Epiphany—Monday St. Michael & All Angels—Evening Prayer	1 Epiphany—Monday St. Michael & All Angels—Evening Prayer
1:1–13	630	Thanks to God whose Word was spoken	,,　　　,,	,,　　　,,
1:1–12	83 97 108	O come, all ye faithful (st. 2) Dost thou in a manger lie Now yield we thanks and praise	,,　　　,,	,,　　　,,
1:3–7	383, 384	Fairest Lord Jesus	,,　　　,,	,,　　　,,
1:3	364 366 421 481	O God, we praise thee, and confess Holy God, we praise thy Name All glory be to God on high Rejoice, the Lord is King	,,　　　,,	,,　　　,,
1:6	93	Angels, from the realms of glory	,,　　　,,	,,　　　,,
2:1–18	448, 449 452	O love, how deep, how broad, how high Glorious the day when Christ was born	See below	See below
2:5–9	450, 451	All hail the power of Jesus' Name	Last Epiphany—Tuesday Ascension Day Annunciation—Morning Prayer	1 Epiphany—Tuesday Ascension Day Annunciation—Morning Prayer

Lectionary A	Lectionary B	Lectionary C	Pastoral Offices & Episcopal Services	Book of Occasional Services	Lesser Feasts and Fasts
See below	See below	See below		See below	
Christmas Day III	Christmas Day III	Christmas Day III		Christmas Festival	
,, ,,	,, ,,	,, ,,		,, ,,	
,, ,,	,, ,,	,, ,,		,, ,,	
,, ,,	,, ,,	,, ,,		,, ,,	
,, ,,	,, ,,	,, ,,		,, ,,	
,, ,,	,, ,,	,, ,,		,, ,,	
The Presentation	Proper 22 The Presentation	The Presentation			
	Proper 22				

			Daily Office Year One	Daily Office Year Two
2:9	455, 456 458 483	O Love of God, how strong and true My song is love unknown The head that once was crowned with thorns	See Above	See Above
2:14–18	142 150	Lord, who throughout these forty days Forty days and forty nights	1 Christmas 1 Lent—Monday Ascension Day Eve of the Visitation	1 Epiphany—Wednesday 1 Lent—Sunday Ascension Day Eve of the Visitation
2:17—10:25	310, 311 327, 328 460, 461	O saving Victim, opening wide Draw nigh and take the Body of the Lord Alleluia! sing to Jesus (st. 4)	See below	See below
2:18	559	Lead us, heavenly Father, lead us	1 Lent—Monday Ascension Day Eve of the Visitation	1 Epiphany—Wednesday 1 Lent—Sunday Ascension Day Eve of the Visitation
3:12–13	697	My God, accept my heart this day	1 Lent—Wednesday	1 Epiphany—Friday
4:9–11	48	O day of radiant gladness	1 Lent—Thursday 1 Lent—Friday Holy Saturday	1 Epiphany—Saturday Holy Saturday
4:14–16	219	The Lord ascendeth upon high	1 Lent—Friday Holy Saturday 6 Easter—Friday	2 Epiphany—Monday
4:15	492 559	Sing, ye faithful, sing with gladness Lead us, heavenly Father, lead us	,, ,,	,, ,,

Lectionary A	Lectionary B	Lectionary C	Pastoral Offices & Episcopal Services	Book of Occasional Services	Lesser Feasts and Fasts
	See Above				
The Presentation	Proper 22 The Presentation	The Presentation			
See below	See below	See below			
The Presentation	Proper 22 The Presentation	The Presentation			
				New Year's Eve	
	Proper 24				
	" "				

			Daily Office Year One	Daily Office Year Two
5:1–10	219 443	The Lord ascendeth up on high From God Christ's deity came forth	1 Lent—Saturday 6 Easter—Friday 6 Easter—Saturday	2 Epiphany—Monday 2 Epiphany—Tuesday
5:7–9	455, 456	O Love of God, how strong and true	1 Lent—Saturday 6 Easter—Saturday	2 Epiphany—Tuesday
7:1—10:25	443	From God Christ's deity came forth	See below	See below
7:11–28	174	At the Lamb's high feast we sing	7 Easter—Wednesday 7 Easter—Thursday	2 Epiphany—Friday
7:26—8:26	219	The Lord ascendeth up on high	7 Easter—Thursday 7 Easter—Friday	2 Epiphany—Saturday 3 Epiphany—Monday
8:1	364 366 421	O God, we praise thee, and confess Holy God, we praise thy Name All glory be to God on high	7 Easter—Friday	3 Epiphany—Monday
9:11—10:39	337 338	And now, O Father, mindful of the love Wherefore, O Father, we thy humble servants	See below	See below
9:11–28	160 219 686	Cross of Jesus, cross of sorrow The Lord ascendeth up on high Come, thou fount of every blessing	7 Easter—Saturday	3 Epiphany—Tuesday 3 Epiphany—Wednesday
9:15	368	Holy Father, great Creator		3 Epiphany—Wednesday
9:23–26	307	Lord, enthroned in heavenly splendor		,, ,,

Lectionary A	Lectionary B	Lectionary C	Pastoral Offices & Episcopal Services	Book of Occasional Services	Lesser Feasts and Fasts
	5 Lent		Ordination: Bishop		
	,,　　,,		,,　　,,		
	See below				
	Proper 26				
	,,　　,,				
See below	See below	See below			See below
Wednesday in Holy Week	Wednesday in Holy Week Proper 27	Wednesday in Holy Week			
,,　　,,	Wednesday in Holy Week	,,　　,,			
,,　　,,	Wednesday in Holy Week Proper 27	,,　　,,			

			Daily Office Year One	Daily Office Year Two
10:1–22	307	Lord, enthroned in heavenly splendor	3 Epiphany—Sunday	3 Epiphany—Thursday 3 Epiphany—Friday
10:10–22	174 202	At the Lamb's high feast we sing The Lamb's high banquet called to share	,, ,,	,, ,,
10:19–25	686	Come, thou fount of every blessing	,, ,,	3 Epiphany—Friday
10:19–22	219	The Lord ascendeth up on high	,, ,,	,, ,,
10:30–39	53	Once he came in blessing	,, ,,	3 Epiphany—Saturday
11:8–40	393	Praise our great and gracious Lord	January 2 4 Epiphany—Sunday	4 Epiphany—Monday 4 Epiphany—Tuesday 4 Epiphany—Wednesday 4 Epiphany—Thursday
11:13–16	623	O what their joy and their glory must be	January 3 4 Epiphany—Sunday	4 Epiphany—Tuesday
11:23–29	363	Ancient of Days, who sittest throned in glory	January 4	4 Epiphany—Wednesday
11:29	187 425	Through the Red Sea brought at last Sing now with joy unto the Lord	,, ,,	,, ,,
12:1–3	545	Lo! what a cloud of witnesses	January 5 5 Epiphany—Sunday Ash Wednesday	4 Epiphany—Thursday Ash Wednesday 5 Easter—Sunday

Lectionary A	Lectionary B	Lectionary C	Pastoral Offices & Episcopal Services	Book of Occasional Services	Lesser Feasts and Fasts
Good Friday Annunciation	Good Friday Annunciation	4 Advent Good Friday Annunciation			Dame Julian of Norwich
,, ,,	,, ,,	,, ,,			,, ,,
Good Friday	Good Friday	Good Friday			,, ,,
,, ,,	,, ,,	,, ,,			,, ,,
St. Thomas	Proper 28 St. Thomas	St. Thomas			Perpetua and her Companion The Martyrs of Uganda
Monday in Holy Week Independence Day	Monday in Holy Week Independence Day	Monday in Holy Week Proper 14 Independence Day		All Saints' Day	
Independence Day	Independence Day	Proper 14 Independence Day			
Monday in Holy Week Of a Saint I	Monday in Holy Week Of a Saint I	Monday in Holy Week Proper 15 Of a Saint I	Ministration to the Sick	All Saints' Day Public Service of Healing	

			Daily Office Year One	Daily Office Year Two
12:1–2	253	Give us the wings of faith to rise	See Above	See Above
	546	Awake, my soul, stretch every nerve		
12:1	490	I want to walk as a child of the light (st. 3)	,, ,,	,, ,,
	552, 553	Fight the good fight with all thy might		
12:2	364	O God, we praise thee, and confess	,, ,,	,, ,,
	366	Holy God, we praise thy Name		
	421	All glory be to God on high		
	483	The head that once was crowned with thorns		
	495	Hail, thou once despised Jesus		
12:3–11	142	Lord, who throughout these forty days	5 Epiphany—Sunday	4 Epiphany—Friday
	152	Kind Maker of the world, O hear	Ash Wednesday	Ash Wednesday
	574, 575	Before thy throne, O God, we kneel		5 Easter—Sunday
12:5–11	636, 637	How firm a foundation, ye saints of the Lord	,, ,,	,, ,,
12:14	512	Come, gracious Spirit, heavenly Dove (st. 3)	Ash Wednesday	4 Epiphany—Saturday
				Ash Wednesday
				5 Easter—Sunday
12:24	368	Holy Father, great Creator	3 Advent—Sunday	4 Epiphany—Saturday
			Last Epiphany—Sunday	7 Easter—Sunday
13:5	636, 637	How firm a foundation, ye saints of the Lord		5 Epiphany—Monday
13:7–9	614	Christ is the King! O friends upraise		,, ,,

Lectionary A	Lectionary B	Lectionary C	Pastoral Offices & Episcopal Services	Book of Occasional Services	Lesser Feasts and Fasts
See Above	See Above	See Above	See Above	See Above	
,, ,,	,, ,,	,, ,,	,, ,,	,, ,,	
,, ,,	,, ,,	,, ,,	,, ,,	,, ,,	
Monday in Holy Week	Monday in Holy Week	Monday in Holy Week Proper 15			William Laud
		Proper 15			,, ,,
		,, ,,			,, ,,
		Proper 16			Augustine of Hippo
		Proper 17			
		,, ,,			

			Daily Office Year One	Daily Office Year Two
13:10–12	219	The Lord ascendeth up on high		See Above
13:12	167	There is a green hill far away		,, ,,
13:15	665	All my hope on God is founded		,, ,,
13:20–21	478 708	Jesus, our mighty Lord Savior, like a shepherd lead us		5 Epiphany—Tuesday

James:

			Daily Office Year One	Daily Office Year Two
1:2–12	636, 637	How firm a foundation, ye saints of the Lord	6 Easter—Monday Proper 7—Sunday	6 Easter—Sunday Proper 27—Thursday
1:12	561	Stand up, stand up for Jesus	,, ,,	Proper 27—Thursday
1:17	291 416	We plow the fields, and scatter For the beauty of the earth	6 Easter—Tuesday Proper 7—Sunday	6 Easter—Sunday Proper 27—Friday
1:22–27	610 628	Lord, whose love through humble service Help us, O Lord, to learn	6 Easter—Tuesday	Proper 20—Sunday Proper 27—Friday
2:1–13	568	Father all loving, who rulest in majesty	Proper 17—Monday	Proper 27—Saturday

Lectionary A	Lectionary B	Lectionary C	Pastoral Offices & Episcopal Services	Book of Occasional Services	Lesser Feasts and Fasts
Thanksgiving Day	Proper 18 Thanksgiving Day	Thanksgiving Day			
,, ,,	,, ,,	,, ,,			William Tyndale
For Social Justice	Proper 19 For Social Justice	For Social Justice			
,, ,,	,, ,,	,, ,,			

			Daily Office Year One	Daily Office Year Two
2:1–9	602 603, 604	Jesu, Jesu, fill us with your love When Christ was lifted from the earth	See Above	See Above
2:14–26	628	Help us, O Lord, to learn	Proper 17—Tuesday	Proper 28—Monday
2:14–17	610	Lord, whose love through humble service	,, ,,	,, ,,
3:1—5:6	574, 575	Before thy throne, O God, we kneel	Proper 17—Wednesday Proper 17—Thursday Proper 17—Friday	Proper 21—Sunday Proper 28—Tuesday Proper 28—Wednesday Proper 28—Thursday
4:6–10	656	Blest are the pure in heart	Proper 17—Thursday	Proper 28—Wednesday
5:1–6	582, 583	O holy city, seen of John	Proper 17—Friday	Proper 28—Thursday

1 Peter:

			Daily Office Year One	Daily Office Year Two
1:3	472	Hope of the world, thou Christ of great compassion	Proper 29—Monday St. Thomas—Morning Prayer	2 Easter—Monday St. Thomas—Morning Prayer
1:18–21	59	Hark! a thrilling voice is sounding	Good Friday Proper 29—Tuesday	Good Friday 2 Easter—Tuesday

Lectionary A	Lectionary B	Lectionary C	Pastoral Offices & Episcopal Services	Book of Occasional Services	Lesser Feasts and Fasts
See Above	See Above	See Above			
For Social Justice World Hunger (GC 82)	Proper 19 For Social Justice World Hunger (GC 82)	For Social Justice World Hunger (GC 2)			
,, ,,	,, ,,	,, ,,			
	Proper 20 Proper 21			Rogation Procession	
	Proper 20			Rogation Procession	
	Proper 21				
2 Easter					The Martyrs of Lyons
3 Easter					

			Daily Office Year One	Daily Office Year Two
1:18–19	524 525	I love thy kingdom, Lord The Church's one foundation	See Above	See Above
1:19	613	Thy kingdom come, O God	,, ,,	,, ,,
1:23–25	204	Now the green blade riseth	Proper 29—Tuesday	2 Easter—Tuesday
2:4–8	518 525	Christ is made the sure foundation The Church's one foundation	2 Easter—Sunday Eve of Pentecost Proper 29—Wednesday	2 Easter—Wednesday Eve of Pentecost
2:9–10	51 59 536	We the Lord's people, heart and voice uniting Hark! a thrilling voice is sounding God has spoken to his people	,, ,,	,, ,,
2:21–25	478 708	Jesus, our mighty Lord Savior, like a shepherd lead us	Proper 29—Thursday	2 Easter—Thursday
2:21–24	208	The strife is o'er, the battle done	,, ,,	,, ,,
2:22–24	492	Sing, ye faithful, sing with gladness	,, ,,	,, ,,
2:24–25	158	Ah, holy Jesus, how hast thou offended	,, ,,	,, ,,
3:18—4:6	455, 456	O Love of God, how strong and true	3 Easter—Sunday Proper 29—Friday Holy Cross Day—Evening Prayer	2 Easter—Friday Proper 29—Sunday Holy Cross Day—Evening Prayer
3:18–20	179	"Welcome, happy morning!" age to age shall say	,, ,,	,, ,,

Lectionary A	Lectionary B	Lectionary C	Pastoral Offices & Episcopal Services	Book of Occasional Services	Lesser Feasts and Fasts
See Above					
,, ,,					
,, ,,					
5 Easter Anniversary of the Dedication of a Church	Anniversary of the Dedication of a Church	Anniversary of the Dedication of a Church	Consecration of a Church		
,, ,,	,, ,,	,, ,,	,, ,,		
4 Easter					Edward Bouverie Pusey
,, ,,					,, ,,
,, ,,					,, ,,
,, ,,					,, ,,
See below	See below	See below		Baptism of Our Lord	James Hannington Edmund (GC 85)
6 Easter Of a Martyr I	1 Lent Of a Martyr I	Of a Martyr I	,, ,,		,, ,,

			Daily Office Year One	Daily Office Year Two
3:18	458	My song is love unknown	See Above	See Above
4:5	63, 64 364 366 421	O heavenly Word, eternal Light O God, we praise thee, and confess Holy God, we praise thy Name All glory be to God on high	3 Easter—Sunday Proper 29—Friday	2 Easter—Friday
4:11	548	Soldiers of Christ, arise	3 Easter—Sunday Proper 29—Saturday	2 Easter—Saturday
5:7–10	563	Go forward, Christian soldier	4 Easter—Sunday St. Bartholomew—Evening Prayer	3 Easter—Monday St. Bartholomew—Evening Prayer
5:7	400 552, 553	All creatures of our God and King Fight the good fight with all thy might (st. 3)	,, ,,	,, ,,

2 Peter:

			Daily Office Year One	Daily Office Year Two
1:17–18	129, 130 133, 134 135 136, 137	Christ upon the mountain peak O Light of Light, Love given birth Songs of thankfulness and praise O wondrous type! O vision fair	3 Advent—Tuesday	1 Advent—Tuesday
1:19	6, 7 40, 41 542	Christ, whose glory fills the skies O Christ, you are both light and day Christ is the world's true Light	,, ,,	,, ,,
3:18	298	All who believe and are baptized	2 Advent—Sunday	1 Advent—Thursday

Lectionary A	Lectionary B	Lectionary C	Pastoral Offices & Episcopal Services	Book of Occasional Services	Lesser Feasts and Fasts
See Above	See Above	See Above		See Above	See Above
Holy Saturday	Holy Saturday	Holy Saturday			
For the Ministry III For Social Service	For the Ministry III For Social Service	For the Ministry III For Social Service			
					Antony Cyprian
					Cyprian
The Transfiguration	Last Epiphany The Transfiguration	The Transfiguration			
,, ,,	,, ,,	,, ,,			
2 Advent					

1 John:

			Daily Office Year One	Daily Office Year Two
1:5–7	**490**	I want to walk as a child of the light	2 Easter—Monday	6 Epiphany—Monday 2 Easter—Sunday Proper 1—Monday
1:7–10	**699**	Jesus, Lover of my soul	" "	" "
1:7–9	**693**	Just as I am, without one plea	" "	" "
3:5	**492**	Sing, ye faithful, sing with gladness	7 Epiphany—Sunday 3 Easter—Friday The Presentation—Evening Prayer	6 Epiphany—Friday Proper 1—Friday The Presentation—Evening Prayer
3:14–18	**573**	Father eternal, Ruler of creation	2 Easter—Saturday	6 Epiphany—Saturday Proper 1—Saturday
3:16–18	**610**	Lord, whose love through humble service	" "	" "
3:16	**304** **319** **603, 604**	I come with joy to meet my Lord You, Lord, we praise in songs of celebration When Christ was lifted from the earth	" "	" "
4:7–12	**84**	Love came down at Christmas	Christmas Day 3 Easter—Tuesday	Christmas Day 7 Epiphany—Tuesday Proper 2—Tuesday
4:8–16	**379** **471**	God is Love, let heaven adore him We sing the praise of him who died	" "	" "
4:9	**439**	What wondrous love is this	" "	" "

Lectionary A	Lectionary B	Lectionary C	Pastoral Offices & Episcopal Services	Book of Occasional Services	Lesser Feasts and Fasts
St. John	3 Easter St. John	St. John			Catherine of Siena
,, ,,	,, ,,	,, ,,			,, ,,
,, ,,	,, ,,	,, ,,			,, ,,
	4 Easter				
	5 Easter				Alban
	,, ,,				,, ,,
	,, ,,				,, ,,
Of the Incarnation	6 Easter Of the Incarnation	Of the Incarnation	Marriage	Special Vocation	Nicholas
Of the Incarnation Human Rights (GC 82)	6 Easter Of the Incarnation Human Rights (GC 82)	Of the Incarnation Human Rights (GC 82)	,, ,,	,, ,,	,, ,,
Of the Incarnation	6 Easter Of the Incarnation	Of the Incarnation	,, ,,	,, ,,	,, ,,

			Daily Office Year One	Daily Office Year Two
4:11–21	573	Father eternal, Ruler of creation	See Above	See Above
4:12, 16	576, 577 581 606	God is love, and where true love is Where charity and love prevail Where true charity and love dwell	,,　　　,,	,,　　　,,
4:18	353 700	Your love, O God, has called us here O love that casts out fear	3 Easter—Tuesday	7 Epiphany—Tuesday Proper 2—Tuesday
4:19	689 706	I sought the Lord, and afterward I knew In your mercy, Lord, you called me	,,　　　,,	,,　　　,,
5:6	139	When Jesus went to Jordan's stream (st. 3)	3 Easter—Wednesday St. John—Evening Prayer	7 Epiphany—Wednesday Proper 2—Wednesday St. John—Evening Prayer
5:14–16	518 711	Christ is made the sure foundation Seek ye first the kingdom of God	3 Easter—Thursday	7 Epiphany—Thursday Proper 2—Thursday
5:20–21	408	Sing praise to God who reigns above (st. 3)	,,　　　,,	,,　　　,,

Jude:

8–9	282, 283	Christ, the fair glory of the holy angels (st. 2)		1 Advent—Friday

Lectionary A	Lectionary B	Lectionary C	Pastoral Offices & Episcopal Services	Book of Occasional Services	Lesser Feasts and Fasts
Of the Incarnation Human Rights (GC 82)	6 Easter Of the Incarnation Human Rights (GC 82)	Of the Incarnation Human Rights (GC 82)	See Above	See Above	See Above
Human Rights (GC 82)	6 Easter Human Rights (GC 82)	Human Rights (GC 82)	,, ,,	,, ,,	,, ,,
,, ,,	,, ,,	,, ,,			
,, ,,	,, ,,	,, ,,			
	2 Easter				
	7 Easter			Public Service of Healing	

Revelation:

			Daily Office Year One	Daily Office Year Two
1:1–3	**231, 232**	By all your saints still striving (Saint John)	December 29	2 Advent—Monday
1:3	**536**	God has spoken to his people	,, ,,	,, ,,
1:4–7	**324**	Let all mortal flesh keep silence (st. 2)	December 29 Proper 25—Monday	,, ,,
1:5	**307**	Lord, enthroned in heavenly splendor	,, ,,	,, ,,
1:7	**57, 58**	Lo! he comes, with clouds descending	,, ,,	,, ,,
1:8	**82** **327, 328**	Of the Father's love begotten Draw nigh and take the Body of the Lord	,, ,,	,, ,,
1:18	**194, 195**	Jesus lives! thy terrors now	December 30 Proper 25—Monday	2 Advent—Wednesday
2:7	**536**	God has spoken to his people	January 7	,, ,,
2:10	**561**	Stand up, stand up for Jesus	January 8	2 Advent—Thursday
2:11, 17	**536**	God has spoken to his people	,, ,,	,, ,,
2:28	**6, 7** **40, 41**	Christ, whose glory fills the skies O Christ, you are both light and day	January 9	2 Advent—Friday
2:29	**536**	God has spoken to his people	,, ,,	,, ,,
3:1–6	**547**	Awake, O sleeper, rise from death	January 10	2 Advent—Saturday

Lectionary A	Lectionary B		Lectionary C		Pastoral Offices & Episcopal Services	Book of Occasional Services		Lesser Feasts and Fasts
	Proper 29		2 Easter					
	,,	,,	,,	,,				
	,,	,,	,,	,,		Consecration of Chrism		
	,,	,,	,,	,,		,,	,,	
	,,	,,	,,	,,		,,	,,	
	,,	,,	,,	,,		,,	,,	
			,,	,,				
								Polycarp
								,, ,,

			Daily Office Year One	Daily Office Year Two
3:4–5	356	May choirs of angels lead you	See Above	See Above
3:6	536	God has spoken to his people	,, ,,	,, ,,
3:7	56	O come, O come, Emmanuel	January 11	3 Advent—Monday
3:13	536	God has spoken to his people	,, ,,	,, ,,
3:21	307	Lord, enthroned in heavenly splendor	January 12	3 Advent—Tuesday
3:22	536	God has spoken to his people	,, ,,	,, ,,
4:6–11	235 364 366 367 401	Come sing, ye choirs exultant (st. 2) O God, we praise thee, and confess Holy God, we praise thy Name Round the Lord in glory seated The God of Abraham praise	Proper 25—Tuesday	3 Advent—Wednesday 3 Advent—Thursday Proper 16—Sunday
4:6	460, 461	Alleluia! sing to Jesus (st. 3)	,, ,,	3 Advent—Wednesday Proper 16—Sunday
4:7–8	643	My God, how wonderful thou art	,, ,,	,, ,,
4:8–11	324 362 657	Let all mortal flesh keep silence Holy, holy, holy! Lord God Almighty Love divine, all loves excelling	,, ,,	3 Advent—Wednesday 3 Advent—Thursday Proper 16—Sunday
4:8	48	O day of radiant gladness	,, ,,	3 Advent—Wednesday Proper 16—Sunday

Lectionary A	Lectionary B	Lectionary C	Pastoral Offices & Episcopal Services	Book of Occasional Services	Lesser Feasts and Fasts
		Trinity Sunday			
	,, ,,				
	,, ,,				
	,, ,,				
	,, ,,				

			Daily Office Year One	Daily Office Year Two
4:11	25, 26	O gracious Light, Lord Jesus Christ	See Above	3 Advent—Thursday
	36	O gladsome Light, O grace		Proper 16—Sunday
	37	O brightness of the immortal Father's face		
	302, 303	Father, we thank thee who hast planted		
	495	Hail, thou once despised Jesus		
5:6–14	213	Come away to the skies (st. 5)	Eve of Ascension	3 Advent—Friday
	307	Lord, enthroned in heavenly splendor	Proper 25—Wednesday	Eve of Ascension
	374	Come, let us join our cheerful songs	Proper 25—Thursday	Proper 17—Sunday
	417, 418	This is the feast of victory for our God		
	434	Nature with open volume stands		
	439	What wondrous love is this		
	460, 461	Alleluia! sing to Jesus		
	495	Hail, thou once despised Jesus		
5:12–13	535	Ye servants of God, your Master proclaim	Eve of Ascension	” ”
			Proper 25—Thursday	
6:9–11	240, 241	Hearken to the anthem glorious	Proper 25—Thursday	3 Advent—Saturday
7:3	473	Lift high the cross	Proper 3—Sunday	Proper 24—Monday
	686	Come, thou fount of every blessing	Proper 25—Friday	
	697	My God, accept my heart this day		
7:9–17	231, 232	By all your saints still striving (All Saints' Day and st. 3)	Proper 3—Sunday	Proper 24—Tuesday
			Proper 25—Saturday	Eve of the Patronal Feast
	240, 241	Hearken to the anthem glorious	Eve of the Patronal Feast	
	275	Hark! the sound of holy voices		
	284	O ye immortal throng (sts. 7 & 8)		
	421	All glory be to God on high		
	618	Ye watchers and ye holy ones		
	619	Sing alleluia forth in duteous praise		
	624	Jerusalem the golden		
	625	Ye holy angels bright		

Lectionary A	Lectionary B	Lectionary C	Pastoral Offices & Episcopal Services	Book of Occasional Services	Lesser Feasts and Fasts
		See Above			
Of the Holy Angels	Of the Holy Angels	3 Easter Of the Holy Angels			
,, ,,	,, ,,	,, ,,			
All Saints' Day	All Saints's Day	All Saints' Day		All Saints' Day	
All Saints' Day Of a Martyr II	All Saints' Day Of a Martyr II	4 Easter All Saints' Day Of a Martyr II	Burial	,, ,,	Vincent Alphege Bernard Mizeki The Martyrs of New Guinea

			Daily Office Year One		Daily Office Year Two	
7:9–14	364	O God, we praise thee, and confess	See Above		See Above	
	366	Holy God, we praise thy Name				
7:9–12	434	Nature with open volume stands	,,	,,	,,	,,
	535	Ye servants of God, your Master proclaim				
	643	My God, how wonderful thou art				
7:13–17	286	Who are these like stars appearing	,,	,,	,,	,,
	356	May choirs of angels lead you				
7:14–17	522, 523	Glorious things of thee are spoken	,,	,,	,,	,,
7:14	691	My faith looks up to thee	,,	,,	,,	,,
11:15–18	494	Crown him with many crowns	Proper 26—Tuesday		Proper 25—Tuesday	
12:7–8	282, 283	Christ, the fair glory of the holy angels (st. 2)	Proper 5—Sunday Proper 26—Wednesday		4 Advent—Sunday Proper 25—Thursday	
13:9	536	God has spoken to his people			Proper 25—Friday	
14:1–5	434	Nature with open volume stands	Proper 26—Thursday		Proper 18—Sunday	
	439	What wondrous love is this			Proper 26—Monday	
14:13	287	For all the saints, who from their labors rest	,,	,,	,,	,,
	357	Jesus, Son of Mary				
	358	Christ the Victorious, give to your servants				

Lectionary A	Lectionary B	Lectionary C	Pastoral Offices & Episcopal Services	Book of Occasional Services	Lesser Feasts and Fasts
See Above	See Above	See Above	See Above	See Above	See Above
,, ,,	,, ,,	,, ,,	,, ,,	,, ,,	,, ,,
,, ,,	,, ,,	,, ,,	,, ,,	,, ,,	,, ,,
,, ,,	,, ,,	,, ,,	,, ,,	,, ,,	,, ,,
,, ,,	,, ,,	,, ,,	,, ,,	,, ,,	,, ,,
St. Michael and All Angels	St. Michael and All Angels	St. Michael and All Angels		All Hallows' Eve	

			Daily Office Year One	Daily Office Year Two
15:3–4	181	Awake and sing the song	Proper 6—Sunday	Proper 26—Tuesday
	532, 533	How wondrous and great thy works, God of praise	Proper 26—Friday	
17:14	483	The head that once was crowned with thorns	Proper 26—Saturday	Proper 26—Friday
	596	Judge eternal, throned in splendor		
19:1–9	434	Nature with open volume stands	Proper 27—Thursday	Trinity Sunday
	439	What wondrous love is this		Proper 27—Tuesday
19:1–8	619	Sing alleluia forth in duteous praise	" "	" "
19:6–9	51	We the Lord's people, heart and voice uniting	" "	" "
	61, 62	"Sleepers, wake!" A voice astounds us		
	174	At the Lamb's high feast we sing		
	202	The Lamb's high banquet called to share		
	300	Glory, love, and praise, and honor		
	316, 317	This is the hour of banquet and of song		
	339	Deck thyself, my soul, with gladness		
	340, 341	For the bread which you have broken		
19:9	213	Come away to the skies (st. 4)	" "	" "
19:16	483	The head that once was crowned with thorns	Proper 27—Friday	Holy Name Trinity Sunday
	596	Judge eternal, throned in splendor		Proper 26—Wednesday
21:1–4	358	Christ the Victorious, give to your servants	4 Advent—Tuesday Eve of Holy Name Proper 28—Tuesday Eves of Apostles and Evangelists	Eve of Holy Name Eves of Apostles and Evangelists

Lectionary A	Lectionary B	Lectionary C	Pastoral Offices & Episcopal Services	Book of Occasional Services	Lesser Feasts and Fasts
Of the Holy Eucharist	Of the Holy Eucharist	5 Easter Of the Holy Eucharist			
,, ,,	,, ,,	,, ,,			
,, ,,	,, ,,	,, ,,			
,, ,,	,, ,,	,, ,,			
Holy Innocents	Holy Innocents	Holy Innocents	Burial Consecration of a Church	New Year's Eve	Martin Luther King (GC 82)

			Daily Office Year One	Daily Office Year Two
21:2—22:5	582, 583 621, 622 623 624	O holy city, seen of John Light's abode, celestial Salem O what their joy and their glory must be Jerusalem the golden	See below	See below
21:2–27	354 356 518 519, 520	Into paradise may the angels lead you May choirs of angels lead you Christ is made the sure foundation Blessed city, heavenly Salem	,, ,,	,, ,,
21:4	566 691	From thee all skill and science flow My faith looks up to thee (st. 3)	4 Advent—Tuesday Eve of Holy Name Proper 28—Tuesday Eves of Apostles and Evangelists	Eve of Holy Name Eves of Apostles and Evangelists
21:6	82	Of the Father's love begotten	4 Advent—Tuesday Eve of Holy Name Proper 28—Tuesday	Eve of Holy Name
21:19–27	61, 62	"Sleepers, wake!" A voice astounds us	4 Advent—Wednesday 4 Advent—Thursday Proper 28—Wednesday Proper 28—Thursday	Epiphany
21:22–27	366	Holy God, we praise thy Name	4 Advent—Thursday Epiphany Proper 28—Thursday	,, ,,
21:23–26	119	As with gladness men of old (sts. 4 & 5)	,, ,,	,, ,,
21:23–25	452	Glorious the day when Christ was born	,, ,,	,, ,,

Lectionary A	Lectionary B	Lectionary C	Pastoral Offices & Episcopal Services	Book of Occasional Services	Lesser Feasts and Fasts
See Above	See Above	6 Easter Holy Innocents	See Above	See Above	See Above
,,　　　,,	,,　　　,,	,,　　　,,	,,　　　,,	,,　　　,,	,,　　　,,
,,　　　,,	,,　　　,,	Holy Innocents	,,　　　,,	,,　　　,,	,,　　　,,
,,　　　,,	,,　　　,,	,,　　　,,	,,　　　,,	,,　　　,,	,,　　　,,
		6 Easter		,,　　　,,	,,　　　,,
		,,　　　,,		,,　　　,,	,,　　　,,
		,,　　　,,		,,　　　,,	,,　　　,,
		,,　　　,,		,,　　　,,	,,　　　,,

			Daily Office Year One	Daily Office Year Two
21:23	**490** **672**	I want to walk as a child of the light O very God of very God	See Above	See Above
22:1–5, 17	**275**	Hark! the sound of holy voices	4 Advent—Thursday December 24 Proper 28—Thursday Proper 28—Saturday	
22:1	**244** **460, 461**	Come, pure hearts, in joyful measure (st. 2) Alleluia! sing to Jesus (st. 3)	4 Advent—Thursday Proper 28—Thursday	
22:3–5	**240, 241** **576, 577**	Hearken to the anthem glorious God is love, and where true love is	,, ,,	
22:3	**535**	Ye servants of God, your Master proclaim	,, ,,	
22:4	**297**	Descend, O Spirit, purging flame	,, ,,	
22:5	**6, 7** **452**	Christ, whose glory fills the skies Glorious the day when Christ was born	,, ,,	
22:13	**82**	Of the Father's love begotten	December 24 Proper 28—Friday	
22:16	**6, 7** **40, 41** **496, 497** **542** **613**	Christ, whose glory fills the skies O Christ, you are both light and day How bright appears the Morning Star Christ is the world's true Light Thy kingdom come, O God	December 24 Proper 28—Saturday	

Lectionary A	Lectionary B	Lectionary C	Pastoral Offices & Episcopal Services	Book of Occasional Services	Lesser Feasts and Fasts
		See Above		See Above	See Above
		,, ,,			,, ,,
		,, ,,			
		,, ,,			,, ,,
		,, ,,			,, ,,
		,, ,,			,, ,,
		,, ,,			,, ,,
		7 Easter			
		,, ,,			

			Daily Office Year One	Daily Office Year Two
22:20	**73**	The King shall come when morning dawns	4 Advent—Friday Proper 28—Saturday	

Lectionary A	Lectionary B	Lectionary C	Pastoral Offices & Episcopal Services	Book of Occasional Services	Lesser Feasts and Fasts
		See Above			